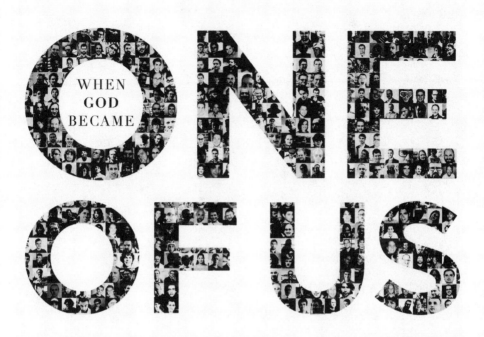

WHEN
GOD
BECAME

ONE
OF US

BRIAN BRODERSEN

40 *Day Journey*
THROUGH THE GOSPEL OF
JOHN

BACK TO
B2B BASICS

P.O. Box 8000, Costa Mesa, CA 92628 • Web: www.backtobasics.com • 1-800-733-6443

When God Became One of Us
A 40-Day Journey Through the Gospel of John

Copyright © 2014 by Brian Brodersen

Published by Back to Basics
P.O. Box 8000
Costa Mesa, CA 92628

First printing 2014

All Scripture quotations, unless otherwise indicated, are taken from the New King James Version®. Copyright ©1982 by Thomas Nelson, Inc. Used by permission. All rights reserved.

Italics in Scripture quotations are the emphasis of the author.

Verses in quotations without references are paraphrases by the author.

To order copies of this book and other Back to Basics products in bulk quantities, please contact us at 1-800-733-6443.

Cover layout and internal design: Aric Everson

Internal layout: Toni Rich

We would especially like to thank Becky English for her editorial skill. Her expertise made this devotional possible.

ISBN: 978-1-59751-936-6

Printed in the United States of America.

CONTENTS

PREFACE

This book came from a series of messages on the gospel of John that I preached at Calvary Chapel Costa Mesa. Its forty entries are condensed versions of those messages, presented in short narratives, for those who desire to know God's Word better but feel daunted at the idea of wading through a lengthy sermon or a massive commentary.

When God Became One of Us can be used as a daily devotional, or it can be read weekly or over a longer period. Each entry contains a portion of Scripture for you to read, some thoughts on the Scripture passage, an opportunity to apply the teaching, and a prayer. You will get the most out of each day's reading if you first read the Bible passage listed at the top of the entry and then read the entry itself.

The purpose of this little book is to provide a fresh look at the person of Jesus through an engaging overview of the gospel of John and to draw the reader to a deeper, personal relationship with Christ and a greater hunger to know and serve Him. I hope as well that this devotional will increase your desire to dig deeper into the Word of God on your own.

Brian Brodersen
Calvary Chapel Costa Mesa, California

GETTING BACK TO JESUS

These are written that you may believe that Jesus is the Christ, the Son of God,
and that believing you may have life in His name.
John 20:31

An interesting phenomenon has occurred in our society regarding Christianity in recent years: many people have been turned off by the church, viewing it as oppressive and hypocritical—yet some of these same people are intrigued by, and even interested in, Jesus Christ. They find Christians appalling but Jesus appealing.

The church, evidently, has done a poor job of representing the Lord.

If we as believers are going to have a significant and lasting impact on the world in this twenty-first century, we will have to shed a lot of our tradition—what we might call "churchiness"—and get back to Jesus Himself.

Every Christian ought to resemble Jesus more and more with the passing of time. Paul told us this: "We all, with unveiled face, beholding as in a mirror the glory of the Lord, are being transformed into the same image from glory to glory" (2 Cor. 3:18). As we behold the Lord, we are transformed into His image. In this wonderful gospel of John, we will get a fresh look at Jesus and see firsthand what God is like.

THE GOSPEL OF JOHN

Each of the gospel writers had a slightly different perspective of Christ to reveal. John, more than any other gospel writer, reveals the deity of Christ. God Himself, John tells us, became one of us, possessing as His own a full human nature from His conception.

John tells us at the outset that the Word—Jesus—was God (see 1:1). He tells us that Jesus claimed to be the great I AM—the One who had revealed Himself to Moses generations earlier in the burning bush (see Ex. 3). He quotes Jesus as saying, "He who has seen Me has seen the Father" (14:9). And John tells us how Thomas cried out to Jesus, "My Lord and my God!" (20:28).

The content of John's gospel, interestingly, centers around seven signs and seven sayings of Jesus, each one conveying something significant to us about who God is. Jesus performed His first sign when He turned water into wine at a wedding feast (see John 2). Through it Jesus let us know that God wants us to enjoy life. Each of Jesus' signs, like this first one, illustrates an increasing revelation of God.

His seven "I am" sayings do the same. Seven times in the gospel of John, Jesus speaks the words "I am ..." and then adds some description to them. In the gospel of John, Jesus takes to Himself this name, the same name that God used to reveal Himself to Israel, thus showing His deity as well as the all-sufficiency of God.

Another unique aspect of John's gospel is its revelation of the person and ministry of the Holy Spirit. The other gospel writers reference the Holy Spirit, but only in John's gospel do we have teaching from Jesus specifically on the Holy Spirit's person and work (see John 16).

As Jesus reveals His Father to us through signs and sayings and teachings, we notice something meaningful: God is personal. John conveys personal and even intimate inter-changes that Jesus had with others. Matthew, Mark, and Luke record the sayings of Jesus, but John records Jesus' conversations. We see Jesus talking with Nicodemus, with a Samaritan woman, with a woman caught in adultery, with Mary and Martha, with Peter. And He holds numerous discussions with the Pharisees—arguments, really.

At the end of his gospel, John tells us why he wrote his book: "These are written that you may believe that Jesus is the Christ, the Son of God, and that believing you may have life in His name" (20:31). Jesus came to show us God so that we could know Him and believe in Him. And have *life*—life that will overflow to those around us.

GETTING BACK TO JESUS

What about you? Are you living the life that Jesus came to give?

Jesus offers believers the hope of heaven, but He also offers us *abundant* life right now—a life that's exciting and thrilling, a life in the Spirit. When we live abundantly, the Scriptures come alive to us. What we read, we can live out because Jesus came to be actively involved in our lives. He leads and guides us. He speaks to us. He works in us and ministers to people through us. That is abundant life.

> The thief does not come except to steal, and to kill, and to destroy. I have
> come that they may have life, and that they may have it more abundantly
> (John 10:10).

We gain this abundant life by believing in Jesus—not just by acknowledging His reality but by trusting in Him, relying on Him, clinging to Him.

The world is becoming more insane every day. We hear about the possibilities of nuclear holocaust, about Christians being persecuted in other countries, about diseases that could wipe out millions of people, about earthquakes, tsunamis, and hurricanes. On the political and social front, things are going from bad to worse. Perhaps all this bad news has gotten you down. Or maybe you're burdened by the cares of life—going to work, taking care of your family, trying to pay the bills. If we as believers in Jesus are going to impact the world around us, we need a fresh taste of the person of Jesus Christ. We need abundant life.

As you discover Jesus in the gospel of John, may you gain a fresh revelation of who He is. May you be filled to overflowing with His life and be used of Him powerfully in these days in which we live.

THE WORD BECAME FLESH

If we were to write someone's biography, we would naturally begin with the person's birth. But for one person in history, life did not begin at birth. Jesus Christ, before being conceived of the Holy Spirit and born of the virgin, Mary, preexisted eternally with the Father.

As John begins to pen his record of Jesus' ministry, he pulls back the veil to reveal the true nature of Jesus Christ: "In the beginning was the Word" (1:1). This is deliberately reminiscent of Genesis 1:1, "In the beginning God ...." Since John's gospel is all about a new beginning, a new creation, John uses words that recall the first creation.

Like the first, this second creation was not carried out by some subordinate being but by the Word, the *Logos*—Jesus Christ, the living Word of God. A word is a revelation, a thought communicated. God, in creating the world, communicated something of who He is. When Jesus came to earth, God spoke again—this time in the form of a man.

This Word, John tells us, was *with* God—in intimate association with God—and the Word *was* God. But the Word was not God the Father; He was God the Son. Herein is a picture of God's plurality—what we refer to as the Trinity—as well as of the deity of Christ.

All that is true of God is true also of the Word. Some have incorrectly translated verse 1, "In the beginning was the Word, and the Word was with God, and the Word was divine." We use the word "divine" rather loosely to describe pleasant music or a delicious dessert. But John is not saying that Jesus is merely divine. He is affirming blatantly, boldly, unashamedly that Jesus, the Word, is none other than God.

If that affirmation is staggering to us, it was more so to the Jewish author of this gospel. For the Jews of John's day, monotheism—the belief that there is only One God— was a conviction clung to and defended with fierce tenacity. John could, of course, say nothing else: he was writing under the inspiration of the Spirit.

John goes on to write that "the Word became flesh and dwelt among us" (1:14)—one of the most profound statements ever made. John is claiming that God became a man.

What would we know of God if Jesus had not come? Not much. We would know that He is an awesome creator. We would know from Old Testament history that He is a righteous judge. We might also know that God has interacted with a small segment of humanity—the nation of Israel. But because Jesus came, we have a more complete picture of who God is.

Under the Old Testament covenant, God struck fear into the people's hearts at Mount Sinai so that they would not sin (see Ex. 20:20). But under the new covenant made known to us in Jesus, we don't come to a mountain burning with fire and smoke. We come to the heavenly Jerusalem (see Heb. 12:18-24)—to a joyful relationship with God. All because the Word became flesh.

During the three years Jesus spent with His disciples, they didn't fully grasp who He was. They were often baffled. There were moments when it seemed as if they were about to get it, but then ... no, not yet.

Imagine John, who spent three years with Jesus but never really understood who He was until after Jesus returned to heaven, many years later writing his gospel and looking back. "The Word became flesh and dwelt among us, *and we beheld His glory*" (1:14). John is describing his own experience. Now he gets it! He knows exactly who was among them. As he looks back at the past events in light of the truth, John is amazed that Jesus is God. *That's who we were with! That's who we walked and talked with!*

May the revelation of who Jesus is break upon us in the same way—and transform our lives.

 ## APPLICATION

 ## PRAYER

How well do you know Jesus? Is your relationship with Him living and vital, or do you need a fresh revelation of who He is? Ask the Lord today to shine His light into your heart and to fill you with the wonder of knowing Him.

Lord, thank You for sending the Word—Jesus Christ, God the Son. Thank You for revealing Yourself to us through Him. As we look for You in the gospel of John, may we see You and be amazed by You and come to love You as never before. In Jesus' name. Amen.

AS MANY AS RECEIVED HIM

Within every one of us is an innate desire for spiritual reality. We all want life and peace. Yet apart from Jesus, we are in darkness—our sin blinds us. How does a person come to know God?

Before Jesus came, God bore universal witness of Himself. He could be seen *above*: "The heavens declare the glory of God" (Ps. 19:1). He could be seen *around* mankind in the amazing creation. And He could be seen *inside* people—in their sense of His existence and their awareness of right and wrong, instilled within them not by parents or culture but by God Himself.

But at a certain point in history, God sent "the true Light which gives light to every man" (1:9), the Lord Jesus Christ, to reveal Himself more fully to man. Into our darkness Jesus brought light—light that enabled us to hear the gospel, respond to the gospel, and believe in the gospel. Good news!

But not everyone was thrilled with Jesus' revelation. Incredibly, although "the world was made through Him, ... the world did not know Him" (1:10). What an indictment! Nature knew Him: the wind, the fish in the sea, even the stones. But the pinnacle of creation—the only creature made in the image of God—refused to acknowledge his Creator. Unbelievable!

Perhaps we could excuse the Gentile world for failing to know Jesus, since for millennia they were left without any specific revelation. But we can never understand how the Jews missed Him. The Jews knew that the Messiah would be a Son of David (see Jer. 23:5), that He would be born in Bethlehem (see Mic. 5:2), and that He would come 173,880 days after the decree to rebuild Jerusalem (see Dan. 9:25). Daniel had also made it clear that the Messiah would be "cut off"—put to death—before the temple was destroyed (see Dan. 9:26), which happened in AD 70. Jesus fulfilled each of these prophecies.

Jesus did other things that the prophets said would mark the messianic age: He healed the deaf and the mute. He gave sight to the blind. He caused the lame to leap for joy. But amazingly, when Jesus healed a man born blind, it provoked intense opposition from the religious leaders (see John 9). Jesus "came to His own, and His own did not receive Him" (1:11).

But here's the hinge: "But as many as received Him ..." (1:12). Israel's rejection of Jesus did not thwart the Messiah's work. The Jews did not recognize Jesus, but God's plan was undeterred. He spoke prophetically of Jesus through the prophet Isaiah, "You will restore Jacob and bring back Israel, and I will also make You a light to the Gentiles" (see Isa. 49:1–6).

"As many as received Him" includes the Gentile nations. Because the Jews rejected their Messiah, God extended salvation to the ends of the earth—which includes you and me. To as many as would receive Him, "He gave the right to become children of God" (1:12).

Not all people are God's children. God is the Creator of all men, but He is the Father only of those who receive Jesus Christ. Jesus is the only One who can give a person the right to become a child of God. We are born in sin, under the judgment of God, and we must be born out of that state (see Eph. 2). We must be born again. This birth is not passed down through the bloodline, nor is it the result of a fleshly determination or the will of man. It is God who gives new life.

We are born again by receiving Christ—the only human component of salvation. We must exercise our will and say, "Jesus, I want You to be my Lord." When we do that, we become children of God—all because the true Light that gives light to every man came into the world.

 ## APPLICATION

 ## PRAYER

Has Jesus opened your eyes to the light? Have you received Him as Lord? If you haven't, will you ask Jesus to open your heart to receive Him and cause you to be born again? If you have, thank God for His precious gift of new life and surrender afresh to Him today.

Lord, thank You for coming to earth and for giving light to each of us. Thank You for giving us the ability to receive You. Help us to recognize You and to receive You so that we can be born again, children of God in this dark world. Amen.

THE TABERNACLE OF GOD IS WITH MEN

Trying to please the Lord isn't always as easy as we might like. Inevitably we fall short in our efforts. But God sent Jesus to meet us at our point of need.

John 1:14 tells us that "the Word became flesh and dwelt among us." The word "dwelt" means "to tabernacle among" or "to pitch one's tent among." It refers back to Exodus: "The glory of the LORD filled the tabernacle" (Ex. 40:34). Moses' tabernacle was indeed a dwelling place for God, but it was also a prophetic visualization of the Word, Jesus Christ, becoming flesh and dwelling among us.

The tabernacle, where man could meet with God and worship Him, was humble in exterior, but what made it significant was that the glory of God resided on it. And so it was with Jesus. He was humble in appearance, but the glory of God emanated forth from Him.

That glory has significant impact on our efforts to please God.

John tells us that the glory of Jesus was "full of grace and truth" (1:14). Grace is our greatest spiritual need. We have no hope of saving ourselves or of working our way into God's favor, which we figure out when we try. But the grace of God enables us to live to His glory. We can stop striving and rest in God's grace.

If grace is our greatest spiritual need, then truth is our greatest practical need. Grace gives us the *strength* to live for God; truth shows us the *way* we are to live for God. Trying to live without truth leads to self-indulgence, which leads ultimately to anarchy.

But the glory of Jesus gets better. From Jesus' fullness we receive "grace for grace" (1:16)—an endless supply of grace. We don't get grace just once for salvation—we can go to God to be replenished over and over as we grow in our relationship with Christ.

Life and grace and truth are found in Jesus Christ. Not in church or duty or a bunch of rules but in relationship with Jesus. The Lord draws us to Himself, saying, "Come to

Me, all you who are weary. I will give you rest" (see Matt. 11:28). As we spend time with Him, He will reveal Himself to us.

The Old Testament law revealed only part of the truth: it spoke of the inflexibility of God's requirements and of the judgment for those who sinned. When Jesus came, He brought God's plan of grace and truth out into the open. Jesus disclosed to us that God Himself would fulfill the requirements of the Law, keep them perfectly, and give His life as a sacrifice for sinners—for us. Apart from the revelation of the New Testament, the Old Testament is an unsolvable riddle. The missing piece of the puzzle, Jesus, is discovered in the New Testament.

Jesus showed us God. In the Greek, John 1:18 says, "The only begotten *God* ... has declared Him"—a clear reference to the deity of Jesus. The Greek word translated "declared" is similar to the word "exposition," which means to bring things out in the open, to help people understand them. Jesus, Himself God, has brought God out into plain view for us. When we see Jesus—His life, His grace, His truth, His rest—we see God.

The men of Jesus' day had the brief experience of God tabernacling with them. And of course, by His Spirit God is with us still today. But just as the tabernacle foreshadowed Jesus' first coming, so the Word becoming flesh and dwelling among us foreshadows more yet to come: "Behold, the tabernacle of God is with men, and He will dwell with them, and they shall be His people" (Rev. 21:3).

One day the tabernacle will be permanent among men, and we will dwell in the Lord's presence, at rest in His unlimited supply of grace, forever.

 ## APPLICATION

Are you trying to please God by following rules, or are you living in the fullness of His grace? The supply of God's grace is endless. Spend time with the Lord today and ask Him for a fresh dose of "grace upon grace" to help you live for His glory.

 ## PRAYER

Lord, thank You that You are full of grace and truth. We need a fresh dose of Your grace poured upon us, and we need Your truth established in us to guide us in this mixed-up world. Lord, we give ourselves to You. Help us to know You as You desire to know us. In the name of Jesus. Amen.

THE SILENCE IS BROKEN

How do you feel when you're promised something and end up waiting a long time for the promise to be kept? Seasons of silence can rattle our nerves—and stretch our faith.

The Jewish people knew about waiting. In 538 BC the Jews, who had been captive in Babylon for seventy years, began returning to Israel. Their long punishment over, they anticipated the coming of God's promised Messiah. This deliverer would save Israel from her enemies, reestablish the Davidic kingdom, and usher in an everlasting reign of righteousness and peace.

But things didn't go as the Jews hoped.

About one hundred years after their return from Babylon, the ministry of the prophets, which had been consistent since the time of Moses, ceased. After Malachi, the nation heard no prophetic word for 400 years.

Things went from bad to worse. Rather than the Davidic kingdom being restored, the brutal Romans ruled over and oppressed the Jews. The priesthood became thoroughly corrupted. Temple worship was reduced to a money-making venture. The spiritual leaders of Israel became an elite group of rigid, merciless legalists who turned the worship of God into an endless list of rules and placed an intolerable burden on the people.

But God hadn't forgotten His promise.

Into the desperate condition of the Jewish nation, a voice cried out. John the Baptist, a wild-looking man who ate honey and wore animal skins, began preaching in the desert. John the Baptist, an unlikely messenger, began telling the Jews about the true Light that was coming into the world. This Light, he told them, would give light to all men.

People flocked to hear him. The Jewish leaders, however, weren't so sure about John. As far as they were concerned, nobody had permission to do anything spiritually without their consent. So they sent priests to ask him, "Who are you?" (1:19).

John answered from the prophet Isaiah: "I am 'The voice of one crying in the wilderness: "Make straight the way of the LORD"'" (1:23). It is worth noting that Malachi, the last prophetic voice to the nation, had also, like Isaiah, spoken of this herald who would announce the Messiah's arrival (see Mal. 3:1). When God's silence was broken, this herald's voice was the first one that the nation heard.

As he preached, John baptized people. The Greek word for "baptism" is *baptizo*. It literally means "to dip" or "to die." Metaphorically, it meant to change identity, appearance, or even relationships. By inviting people to be baptized, John was calling them to repent of their sins and to renew their relationship with God—the very reason the Messiah was coming into the world.

One day as Jesus walked toward John the Baptist, John called to the people, "Behold! The Lamb of God who takes away the sin of the world!" (1:29). John was making clear that Jesus' coming was not just for the Jew but also for the Gentile.

Israel's response to the breaking of God's silence was mixed.

The Jews expected the Messiah to be primarily a conqueror. The last thing they thought they needed was someone to deal with their sin. They expected the Messiah to conquer the oppressive Roman government and set up a worldwide Jewish kingdom.

But Jesus came first and foremost to be a Savior. And many who heard John's message believed, repented, and were baptized—and their lives were changed.

There have been other silent years in the history of God's people. During another 400-hundred-year period, the family of Israel labored as slaves in Egypt. Later, during the silence of the Dark Ages, God awakened Martin Luther to the power of God's Word, and a great revolution broke out all over Europe.

When God intervenes, it's powerful. His answers may surprise us, but they are ultimately and always for our salvation.

 ## APPLICATION

 ## PRAYER

If God has been silent toward you, keep waiting and watching. God has precise timing for His plans, and He will be faithful to keep His promise in your life. The silence will break, as it did for Israel. God will speak and blessings will flow.

Father, thank You for Your promises. As we remember the start of the Lord Jesus' ministry, we are reminded that You keep Your promises. Thank You for Jesus, the Lamb of God who took away our sin— the fulfillment of Your promise to us. Even in our seasons of silence, we thank You because we know that You will speak to us. Give us the patience to wait for You. In Jesus' name. Amen.

CALLED TO DISCIPLESHIP

When you hear the word "Christian," what do you think of? Many people today don't have the slightest idea what it means to be a Christian. Being a Christian is more than embracing an intellectual belief—it means following Jesus closely as a disciple.

John the Baptist, the herald of the Messiah, stood one day with two of his disciples as Jesus approached him. As he had done the day before, John called out, "Behold the Lamb of God!" (1:36). Powerful words.

In the late 1800s the famous London pastor Charles Spurgeon spoke at the 20,000-seat Crystal Palace. Before the event Spurgeon tested the acoustics. In the vast auditorium he shouted over and over, "Behold! The Lamb of God who takes away the sin of the world!" Elsewhere in the building, a laborer heard the repeated phrase. For all he knew it was a voice from heaven. Simply from hearing this proclamation, this man gave his life to Jesus Christ.

So it was with these disciples of John the Baptist. Knowing that John was the herald of the Messiah, they rightly concluded from John's statement that Jesus was the Messiah and that they were now to follow Him.

The word "follow" in verse 37, because of its Greek tense, implies that these two men followed Jesus permanently from then on. Too many today follow Jesus for a while and then drift on to other things. Some likely think that this is part of the Christian experience because it happens so frequently. But it never has to be the case. Like these men, we can become disciples of Jesus and never turn back.

Andrew, one of the two who had followed Jesus, found his brother Peter and told him, "We have found the Messiah" (1:41), and he took him to Jesus. Andrew and Peter were common folk—ordinary people. The common people were full of messianic expectation. Ironically, there was little messianic expectation among the religious leaders—at least they didn't speak or write much about it. This is likely because they weren't too anxious for the Messiah to come and disturb their position (see John 11:47–48).

But the common folk had been looking for the Messiah and were ready to follow Him when He called.

It's a beautiful thing that God calls and uses ordinary men and women. Unfortunately, throughout much of church history, the idea of hierarchy has been prevalent. People have believed that God mainly uses pastors and leaders, while the folks in the pew simply watch. But this isn't a biblical picture.

The next day Jesus found Philip, who was from the same town that Andrew and Peter were from, and said to him, "Follow Me" (1:43). Philip in turn found Nathanael and told him, in essence, "We have found the Christ!" Thus the Lord's band of twelve began to form.

Jesus still calls people to be His disciples. As we answer the call to follow Jesus, we end up doing things we would have never dreamed. God may send us to the Philippines, Uganda, France, or elsewhere to minister the gospel and to serve others. And whom does He call? Ordinary people.

God used an ordinary man named John Bunyan. Bunyan was a handyman, yet he felt called by God to minister His Word. He began to preach, but it got him cast into prison for thirteen years. He didn't have much education to speak of, but in prison Bunyan felt inclined to write. He wrote several books, one of them, *The Pilgrim's Progress*, the second bestselling book of all time.

Implied in the word "Christian," or "little Christ," is the idea of discipleship. The word "disciple" means "learner" or "follower." It implies devotion, commitment, and submission to a master. In our culture the term "Christian" no longer means what it originally did. Perhaps it's time that we identify ourselves differently—maybe we should simply call ourselves followers of Jesus. That's what being a Christian is really all about.

 ## APPLICATION

 ## PRAYER

Are you Jesus' disciple? If you've drifted from following the Lord, get back to the place where you should be. Like the disciples did, follow after Jesus. Do it consistently, steadfastly, *permanently*. Now is not the time to be drifting. God is choosing you—and He wants to use you.

Thank You, Lord, for calling us to follow Jesus. There is nothing greater than to know You and follow You and to live out the wonderful plan and purpose that You have for our lives. Help us to make the commitment to follow You fully from this day forward. In Jesus' name. Amen.

THE JOY OF THE LORD

God is so often misrepresented. When Jesus came, this was happening in the extreme. The religious leaders, intent on their own agenda, were burdening people with guilt and condemnation, making God out to be angry with them. But that is not at all the picture of God that Jesus revealed.

In Jesus' day and culture, a wedding could last a week. As my friend Jon Courson writes, "It was sort of a family reunion, a wedding shower, a bachelor party, a wedding, and a honeymoon all rolled into one."[1] At the wedding that Jesus and His disciples attended in Cana, the hosts ran out of wine. This would have been extremely embarrassing, even disgraceful, in Middle Eastern culture. The bridegroom was in a quandary.

When Mary noticed this, she said to Jesus, "They have no wine" (2:3). Mary knew what very few did: her Son was the Messiah. Jesus told His mother, "My hour has not yet come" (2:4). But Mary evidently sensed that Jesus was going to do something. She told the servants standing nearby, "Whatever He says to you, do it" (2:5).

Jesus looked at six large stone water pots and told the servants to fill them with water and then to take some of the contents to the master of ceremonies. They did so, and the master of ceremonies, surprised, told the bridegroom, "You have kept the good wine until now!" (2:10).

John refers to this first miracle of Jesus as a *sign*. Jesus' purpose in using signs was to take people beyond the miracle itself and to show them something behind it—and this is what Jesus did here.

First—and we'll see this throughout the gospel of John—Jesus revealed His divine nature. In creating something from nothing, He did something that only God could. This pointed to His true nature: the Messiah of Israel.

Jesus also showed that God wants to bless people's lives. The religious leaders were hypocrites: the Sadducees were in collusion with the Romans and only wanted money, and the Pharisees were self-righteous legalists. The leaders gave people the impression that God was anxious to judge them because of their weaknesses and failures and sins. In providing wine for the wedding party, Jesus demonstrated God's desire to impart joy to people. God wants to keep us from *destruction*, yes, but not from good things. Jesus came to give us abundant life (see John 10:10). Whenever Jesus comes into a situation or a fellowship or a family or a life, He brings joy and blessing and peace.

Finally, Jesus demonstrated that God uses ordinary objects to do extraordinary things. Until the moment that Jesus pointed to those stone water pots and said, "Fill them with water," it's likely that nobody looked twice at them. There they sat, empty and ill-esteemed, having nothing to do with the décor or function of the festival. But when Jesus made use of them, suddenly what had been totally insignificant became the vehicle through which blessing came.

You might be like those water pots. You might think, *Nobody knows I exist. I come to church every week but sit on the sidelines, overlooked.* The Lord sees you. And at the opportune moment—you never know when—He will suddenly say, "Fill that pot right there."

As ordinary people like you and me are filled up with the water of the Word of God, it brims over from our lives, and God transforms it into the wine of joy. At the given moment in God's sovereign plan, the wine of God's joy and of His Holy Spirit will overflow. From there it will spread and touch the lives of many.

 APPLICATION

 PRAYER

If you feel sad or lonely or overlooked, fill yourself with the Word of God. Let it overflow your life and run over the brim. Then watch and see what happens. The Spirit of God and the joy of the Lord will fill you in a fresh way, and He will overflow from you into the lives of others.

Lord, thank You that You still touch water and turn it into wine. We want to be filled up with You. Let us be people in whom the Word dwells richly so that the Spirit of Christ will overflow from us. We sometimes look for joy in all the wrong places—remind us that You are the giver of joy. Cause Your joy to overflow from us. In Jesus' name. Amen.

ZEAL FOR GOD'S HOUSE

God doesn't like a mess in His house—whether in the church collectively or in Christians individually. Sooner or later, if we don't clean up the clutter in our lives, God will deal with it.

After the wedding in Cana, Jesus and His disciples headed back to Jerusalem for the Passover. But when they entered the temple, happenings there were a far cry from what God intended them to be.

In Jesus' day the high priest, Annas, and his family had set up a marketplace in the temple portico. Jewish historian Josephus says that Annas was a great hoarder of money who by violence robbed the common priests of their official revenues. The temple, dedicated by God as a place of worship, had been turned into a family business.

When a Jew came to worship in Jerusalem, he was to bring a sacrifice or buy one at the temple. But the priests had hiked up the prices astronomically. The moneychangers were just as bad. They inflated the exchange rate for Jewish worshipers from all over the world. The people were being robbed. There is little record in the Scriptures of Jesus being angry, but on this occasion He was.

The exploitation of people goes on in the church today. How many times have we watched so-called Christian leaders on television plead for money and then live extravagantly from it? Other evangelical leaders adapt a business model for ministry and seek to market their product—the gospel. A church *does* have a business element to it, but that aspect should be as low-key as possible and be run by the strictest biblical principles.

When Jesus came to the temple that day, the leaders were ostensibly directing the people in proper sacrifice, but Jesus saw through their deception, and He refined and purified and purged the house of God.

The Jewish leaders were not pleased. "What sign do You show to us, since You do these things?" (2:18). Notice that they didn't say, "You have no business doing this." They knew their behavior was wrong.

Jesus cryptically answered the Jews, "Destroy this temple, and in three days I will raise it up" (2:19). The Jews had no idea what He was talking about, but Jesus was speaking of His own body. His resurrection from the dead would prove His authority to cleanse God's house.

Today, sins of all sorts are tolerated within the church. If we seek to exhort or discipline somebody, we can be threatened with a lawsuit—and the people who refuse correction simply move to the church down the street. Often the lack of spiritual power in the church today is a result of our impurity and our failure to address it. But the Lord will not tolerate sin in His temple.

The Lord deals with us individually as well. He sees our clutter and rubbish and says, "This is a mess. We need to clean up." Jesus will not make His home in a heart given over to sin. He will drive out bad influences and deal with sinful things in our lives.

But first, He makes us an offer: "If we would judge ourselves, we would not be judged [by the Lord]" (1 Cor. 11:31). The Lord doesn't start by aggressively turning over tables. He prefers to say to us, "Let's get rid of that right there," and He wants us to simply respond, "Yes, Lord." Only when we stubbornly refuse to take care of things does God say, "Time's up. Here I come."

If we don't deal with sin, God will, because He doesn't want us to be judged with the world (see 1 Cor. 11:32). But we don't have to let things go that far. We can respond to the conviction of the Spirit.

 ## APPLICATION

 ## PRAYER

Is there anything in your life that God might want you to deal with? Clean it out! Get rid of anything sinful or questionable. Jesus came to Jerusalem to bless, but He could not bless that which was an offense to Him (see Luke 13:34; 19:41). Allow the Lord to do His refining work in your life so that you can receive the blessing He wants to give you.

Thank You, Lord, for cleansing us from things that hinder Your blessing. We lay our hearts open before You and pray that Your Spirit will help us get rid of anything in our lives that needs to be thrown out. Move in us by Your Spirit. In Jesus' name. Amen.

YOU MUST BE BORN AGAIN

People can be religious and not be born again. They can go to church and do the things that people expect Christians to do. What does it mean to be born again?

Jesus, now in Jerusalem, did many more signs, and people believed in Him. But the literal translation of John 2:24 says, "Jesus did not believe in them." Jesus knew that these people were more interested in what He might *do* for them than in who He *was*.

But Nicodemus—he was a different sort. He had an honest interest in Jesus. So to this man Jesus gave an audience. G. Campbell Morgan wrote, "Christ will always give Himself to honesty. If a man in his approach to the Lord, will state his difficulties, Christ is ever ready to receive him."[2]

Nicodemus was a Pharisee, a ruler of the Jews. The Pharisees generally opposed Jesus, but Nicodemus truly loved God and his neighbor. He kept the commandments, and he epitomized ceremonial purity. Later, when the Jewish leaders condemned Jesus, Nicodemus stood against them. And Nicodemus helped bury Jesus after His crucifixion.

But all this wasn't adequate to allow him entrance into heaven.

As they began to talk, the Lord cut right to Nicodemus's heart: "Unless one is born again, he cannot see the kingdom of God" (3:3). It seemed to Nicodemus a strange statement. He asked Jesus, understandably, how an old person could be born a second time.

Jesus didn't answer directly. He told Nicodemus that unless one was born again, he could not see—perceive or comprehend—the kingdom of God (see 1 Cor. 2:14). To understand the things of the kingdom, we must be born again. But, as Nicodemus asked, what does that really mean?

Man was originally created in God's image—spirit, soul, and body—the spirit being uppermost. But when sin brought spiritual death, it essentially reduced man to a two-dimensional being. He was now predominately soul and body.

Still, we hold traces of our spiritual aspect. We are moral beings. We are also worshipers. Some worship false gods, of course, and some claim not to worship God at all. But

24

even atheists worship heroes and ideologies. The fact that man is a moral being who worships shows the remnant of the spirit still within us. Being born again simply means having our spiritually dead part brought back to life by the infusion of the Holy Spirit.

Jesus went on to tell Nicodemus that if a man is not born again, he cannot *see* the kingdom of God, nor can he *enter* it. Some feel that it is harsh to say that those who are not born again will not go to heaven. But it's what Jesus said. Of course, God is drawing people so that they will be born again. But unless a man is born again, he cannot enter the kingdom of God.

Nicodemus was astonished by Jesus' words. He could not grasp them. He was thinking in human terms rather than spiritual.

Isn't that our problem today? We think in terms of what we can see and understand. But a lot of things that we can't see exist. Like the wind. We can only hear it and feel it and see its effects. Jesus says, "So is everyone who is born of the Spirit" (3:8).

Just as we can see the wind's effects, so we can see the effects of being born again: A person who is born again believes that Jesus is the Christ (1 John 5:1). He does not habitually practice sin (1 John 5:18) but instead practices righteousness (1 John 2:29). A born-again believer loves others (1 John 4:7). And he overcomes the world (1 John 5:4).

Salvation is not a reformation or a self-improvement plan but an entirely new life. That's what Jesus came to offer Nicodemus and to us. We must be born again.

 ## APPLICATION

Jesus said, "You *must* be born again." It isn't optional. No one can be a Christian apart from being born again. If Nicodemus, a Jew and a perfect man in many ways, needed more than his goodness to get to heaven, where does that leave you and me? Have you renounced your own goodness and any hope of saving yourself? Are you born again?

 ## PRAYER

Thank You, Lord, that You came into this world so that we could have new life. Being dead in our trespasses and sins, we had no possibility of altering our condition. How we thank You that You did for us what we could never do for ourselves. We embrace Your offer of new life in Jesus' mighty name. Amen.

GOD SO LOVED THE WORLD

Do you ever feel as if God couldn't possibly love you? Maybe you think you're too messed up, that you could never get into the Lord's good graces. But "God so loved the world that He gave His only begotten Son, that whoever believes in Him should not perish but have everlasting life" (3:16). He loves the whole world. You. Me. The worst sinner.

Jesus had told Nicodemus what it means to be born again, and the rabbi then asked Him, "How can these things be?" (3:9). The Lord answered with an Old Testament verse: "As Moses lifted up the serpent in the wilderness, even so must the Son of Man be lifted up, that whoever believes in Him should not perish but have eternal life" (3:14–15).

Jesus was referring to a time when God had punished Israel's rebellion with poisonous fiery serpents. The Israelites had pled for deliverance, and the Lord had told Moses, "Make a fiery serpent, and set it on a pole; and it shall be that everyone who is bitten, when he looks at it, shall live" (Num. 21:8). Jesus was telling Nicodemus, "It's like that. Just as the serpent was lifted up, so I must be lifted up, so that whoever believes in Me will not die but live."

John 3:16, probably the best known and most quoted passage in the Bible, tells us why God sent His Son to "be lifted up." The little word "so" implies that God loved the world so much that the word "love" itself could not adequately express God's heart.

Who is "the world"? Wicked, sinful people. Some think that Jesus was saying God loved "the world of the elect," a small number of people whom God chose to be saved. But the Greek word for "world," *cosmos*, is consistently used in Scripture to describe all people. God loves everybody. And He loves each person individually—whether rich or poor, learned or unlearned, talented or untalented, handsome or homely, strong or weak. Good or bad. You can say to your neighbor, your colleague, the mechanic fixing your car, the person ringing up your groceries, "Do you know that Jesus loves you?"

God's love is not an occasional shout from heaven, "Love you down there! Hope you're all right." No, God demonstrated His love: "God so loved the world that He *gave*." God said, "I love you," and then He said, "I'll show you what I mean."

The words "only begotten" mean "one and only." Jesus Christ is God's Son as nobody else is. Yes, Christians are children of God, but we became sons and daughters of God through faith in Jesus, and Jesus has always been the one and only Son of God. And this Son—His most precious possession—is who God gave.

Now Jesus wraps up His answer to Nicodemus' question. He has told him about God's part in bringing about the new birth: loving and giving. Now Jesus explains the human element to the salvation equation: belief in Him.

The Greek word for "believe" implies action rather than simply intellectual assent. When we believe something with all our heart, we act upon it. To believe in Jesus means to take the facts about Him and apply them to our lives personally—by surrendering to Him, trusting in Him, clinging to Him. Our belief in Him alters our life. This is saving faith.

All who believe in Jesus have eternal life. Nobody needs to perish. We are here on earth to proclaim this wonderful message. A lot of people have a mental picture of Christians as accusers, as holier-than-thou hypocrites, but God didn't send Jesus into the world to condemn it—it's already condemned. Let's be wise and gentle in our approach to people. God sent Jesus into the world to save us—because He loves us.

 APPLICATION

 PRAYER

If you ever doubt that God loves you, remember the cross of Jesus Christ. Our feelings about God's love come and go, but the love of God is a reality that was demonstrated in history and one that we can bank on—and take to the world around us.

Thank You, Lord, that You came to save. Your love for the world hasn't waned because of sin. You still want to save people and draw them to Yourself. Keep extending that grace, we pray, and help us to be instruments of that grace. Let us be extensions of Your love and grace to the people around us. In Jesus' name. Amen.

WHY MEN GO TO HELL

God doesn't look at sinners the way we sometimes do: *How disgusting! What a sinner! They ought to put that guy in jail!* God "desires all men to be saved and to come to the knowledge of the truth" (1 Tim. 2:4), and He wants us to have His heart for the lost.

As Jesus continued His conversation with Nicodemus, He sought to impress on this man God's heart for people. God does everything in His power short of violating our free will to keep us from perishing. He sent Jesus to pay the penalty for sin. He sent the Holy Spirit to convict us of sin and to persuade us to turn to God. And He blesses our lives and orchestrates events in order to get our attention. God's whole program is salvation.

But here's the tragedy: more people will end up in hell than in heaven.

It's a mistake for the church to downplay the seriousness of hell or to inhibit talking about it. Some leading thinkers in what is known as the Emerging Church advocate the idea that we stop talking about personal salvation from hell and realize that the gospel is much grander than that. They believe that we should save society and the planet so that people can live better lives. How dangerously sad. Hell is a reality. And it's where a person is headed if he refuses the grace of God. People need to know that.

But why such a stark punishment?

God never intended it that way. He didn't make hell for people but for the Devil and his angels (see Matt. 25:41). John tells us that people are condemned because they reject Jesus Christ: "He who does not believe is condemned" (3:18). This is heavy. The ultimate condemnation comes not from sin but from rejecting the ultimate light—the light of the gospel.

God has given us light through His creation and through our consciences. He also gives us light through the Scriptures. But when John talks about the light that came into the world, he is referring to the light of the gospel. Jesus, *the* Light of the World.

John tells us that when Jesus came, "men loved darkness rather than light" (3:19). It seems inconceivable to us that people could love darkness. But the Scriptures tell us that people love the darkness of their pride, evil thoughts, stubborn wills, hatred, and lust.

Not only do people love darkness, they are hostile to the light. Our society makes the mistake of thinking that people are innocent, that they are ignorant and need to be enlightened. When a person commits a heinous crime or is involved in some deplorable act, we see them as sick—as victims rather than active collaborators with sin and Satan. But this perspective comes from having our minds diluted by the world rather than influenced by the Word of God. God says, "There is none righteous, no, not one" (Rom. 3:10). Man's natural bent and inclination is to rebel against God.

Why do people reject the light? Can you imagine being lost in a pitch-black mine and telling someone who brings you a light, "No, put that out"? Of course not. But people do it. Why? When a person has been in the dark and suddenly steps into brilliant light, it can be uncomfortable. When we come to people with the light of the gospel, oftentimes the light shocks them. The light exposes their evil.

"But he who does the truth comes to the light, that his deeds may be clearly seen, that they have been done in God" (3:21). To be free of darkness, all we have to do is come to the light. The moment we do, God is full of grace to receive us and to give us eternal life.

 APPLICATION

 PRAYER

How do you view people—criminals, panhandlers, government officials, your insensitive neighbors? Do you see them as people whom God wants to save? God is so unimaginably patient with people, even those who love the darkness and hate the light. Ask the Lord today to give you His love for *all* people and to help you minister to them the light of the gospel.

Thank You, Jesus, that You came into this world to take the punishment for our sins so that we could live with You forever. May we grow in our understanding of Your great love for us and for others. Use us as instruments to spread Your love and truth to those who so desperately need You. In Jesus' name. Amen.

HE MUST INCREASE

Many Christians today are so indoctrinated by the philosophy of the world that we tend to forget what discipleship is all about. We start thinking that things are all about us, and we find it quite strange that the Lord would require any sort of sacrifice from us. But Jesus calls us to self-denial.

Jesus left Jerusalem with His disciples and went to Judea, where He took up the ministry of baptism. When the disciples of John the Baptist noticed that Jesus was baptizing more people than John was, they became zealous for their master. They went to John and said, "The One you pointed to is baptizing, and now everybody is going to Him!" (see John 3:26). But of course, that's why John had come—to point people to Jesus.

These men are so typical of us. We latch on to a favorite pastor or leader and become divided from other Christians over our loyalty to a person. But God is doing something much larger than any one church or group. One of the biggest obstacles to people getting involved in the church is the way Christians bicker and debate and argue—quite often over insignificant things. There are certainly vital issues that we need to stand for and times when we need to rise up against false teaching. But most of the divisions that take place in churches have little or nothing to do with the defense of the faith.

We need strength and unity among Christians today. For this we need to get ourselves out of the way and together look to Jesus. "You yourselves heard me say that I am not the Christ," John told his followers. "I'm like a friend of the bridegroom, and I'm glad that the bridegroom is now center stage!" (see John 3:28-29). John the Baptist, in his humility, beautifully deflected the situation and turned his followers' attention back to the Lord. Like John, we need to point people back to Christ.

"He must increase, but I *must* decrease" (3:30), John emphasized. His answer summarizes the goal of the Christian life: more of Jesus and less of me. Self—not the Devil, not the world—is the greatest obstacle to Christian maturity. Self-centeredness, self-importance, and self-seeking are encouraged and promoted from every conceivable avenue in our day. But Jesus said, "If anyone desires to come after Me, let him deny himself, and take up his cross, and follow Me" (Matt. 16:24).

This applies to our personal lives as well. The Lord may ask us, for the sake of His call on our lives, to deny ourselves the comforts of home or familiarity. We may need to deny ourselves a relationship that is interfering with God's will for us. Perhaps we're called to deny ourselves certain liberties that we enjoy but that could possibly stumble a weaker brother or sister.

Denying ourselves is not always easy. Sometimes it's extremely challenging. But just because something is difficult doesn't mean that God is not in it. He is transforming us into the image of His Son. As we decrease, He increases the presence and the life of Jesus within us.

It is easy for us to get wrapped up in our church and our ministry and practically forget that there are Christians outside our own borders. We can become consumed with the precious plans we have laid for our lives. But everything we do is about the centrality of Jesus Christ. We must fight to keep Him at the center of everything.

John the Baptist was able to do this because he was truly humble. He sought to do nothing but what God had appointed him to do. It's all about Jesus. He must increase. We must decrease.

 APPLICATION

In what area of your life might you need to deny yourself? "I want to increase My presence in your life," the Lord may be saying to you. "I want to work through you, but you are in the way." Deny yourself. Drop that attitude. Open your heart to that brother or sister. Let go of that position. Withdraw from that situation. As you let Christ increase, you will see a blessing in your situation.

 PRAYER

Lord, thank You that You want to manifest Yourself through us. We realize that we have the ability to interfere with that. Forgive us, Lord. If we want to follow You, we must deny ourselves. Let us decrease, Lord, that You might increase and be glorified. In Jesus' name. Amen.

LIVING WATER

So many people today are weary and miserable. If they only knew the gift that God wants to impart to each of us—the gift of Living Water!

Jesus was on His way from Judea to Galilee, and He "needed to go through Samaria" (4:4). The Samaritans, a people of mixed race, were generally looked down upon by the Jews. Orthodox Jews traveled around Samaria to avoid defilement, but Jesus didn't have any such hang-ups. He needed to go through the area for an encounter with someone.

Jesus, tired from traveling, sat down by Jacob's well. His disciples headed into town to buy lunch, and as Jesus rested alone, a woman came to draw water.

A religious Jew would never have talked to a Samaritan, especially a woman. And this woman was a social outcast, even among her own people. The women of the town normally came for water early in the day, but this woman came at midday, likely to avoid disdain over her miserable moral failures. She was, no doubt, empty and weary.

When the woman approached the well, Jesus asked her for a drink. The woman was taken aback. "Why are You, a Jew, asking me, a Samaritan woman, for a drink?"

Jesus seized the moment: "If you knew who was asking you for a drink, you would have asked Him instead—and He would have given you living water."

The woman's reply was skeptical and a bit sarcastic. "Where do You get this living water? Are You greater than our father Jacob?"

"Whoever drinks of this water will thirst again" (4:13), Jesus told her. By "this water" He was referring to the well but also to those things she had pursued in hopes of personal fulfillment. In her case it was relationships—in our case it might be our jobs, money, fame. "But whoever drinks of the water that I shall give him will never thirst" (4:14). In fact, Jesus told the woman, it would spring up inside her into everlasting life.

The woman was interested. "Where do I get it?" she asked.

Jesus, in His typical manner, didn't answer directly. Instead He put His finger on an obstacle in this woman's life: "Go, call your husband, and come here" (4:16).

"I have no husband" (4:17), the woman replied.

Jesus told her, "You're right. You've had five husbands, and the man you have now isn't your husband." The woman suddenly realized that Jesus was no ordinary person.

Jesus addressed this woman's sin, not to condemn her, but that she might receive the blessing He wanted to give her. But upon realizing that Jesus must be some kind of prophet, she immediately retreated from the issue of her sin and into religious discussion.

Jesus wasn't deterred. "God is seeking worshipers," He told her, "who will worship Him in spirit and truth." In other words, the solution for our sin is not religion—it's a relationship with God.

Man was created to worship. But when we worship wrong things—ideologies, relationships, possessions—we end up miserable and, ultimately, destroyed.

The woman said to Jesus, "When Messiah comes, He'll explain things to us."

"Jesus said to her, 'I who speak to you am He'" (4:26). Jesus told this woman openly and unreservedly that He was the Messiah—something He seldom did. And let it be forever remembered that His statement was not made to learned scribes or moral Pharisees but to one who until that moment had been an ignorant, thoughtless, immoral person.

What Jesus Christ said to this woman, He says to us: "If you knew the gift of God, and who it is who says to you, 'Give Me a drink,' you would have asked Him, and He would have given you living water" (4:10). That offer is extended to anyone who is thirsty and who is ready to receive it.

 ## APPLICATION

 ## PRAYER

Are you tired? Empty? Rejected? Are you worshiping anything that will lead to your destruction? No matter how broken you may be or how lonely you feel, Jesus offers you a dynamic relationship, vibrant and overflowing, that will flow out from your life and touch the lives of others. Ask Him for a fresh drink of His living water today.

Thank You, Lord, for this reminder of how You love us. How we thank You, Lord, that Your salvation is for sinners. Thank You that You came to reveal the Father, who is seeking worshipers. May Your living water flow from within us and touch those around us. We thank You, we praise You, we bless You. In Jesus' name. Amen.

THE FIELDS ARE WHITE FOR HARVEST

God wants us to share His love and truth with others, but sometimes we get hung up. *What do I say? Where do I begin?*

Jesus had been speaking to a sinful, broken Samaritan woman about the water of life. As His disciples arrived with food, "they marveled that He talked with a woman" (4:27), a Samaritan woman at that.

But this woman had been so impacted by her encounter with Jesus that she left her water pot and rushed back to town. She told the village, "Come, see a Man who told me all things that I ever did. Could this be the Christ?" (4:29).

For some of us, talking about Christ comes naturally. But it's not as easy for all of us as it seemed to be for the Samaritan woman. Maybe we're shy, or maybe we're worried someone will ask us a question that we can't answer. The Samaritan woman didn't know much, but she knew what God had done for her. Her message was simple yet compelling.

The most effective form of witnessing for Christ is personal evangelism. Crusade evangelism and programs have their place, but nothing can substitute sharing the life of Jesus one-on-one with someone. And sometimes simply relating our own encounter with Christ is the best way to do it.

If each of us went out every week and said, "Lord, use me to share Your love with somebody," we would see many people come to faith in Jesus. The problem is that we get intimidated—and we miss out. We need to start by praying, "Lord, bring about an opportunity," and then when God brings one, we need to speak up.

While the woman was gone, the disciples said, "Lord, here. Eat." But Jesus said to them, "I have food that you don't know about." They looked at each other, saying, "Who brought Him food?" Jesus told His followers, "My food—that which nourishes and satisfies Me—is to do My Father's will and finish His work." Jesus was telling His disciples, "If I need to eat, I'll eat, but I'm taken up with something else right now." He went on to say, "Lift up your eyes and look at the fields, for they are already white for harvest!" (4:35). Jesus wasn't talking about fruits or vegetables. He was talking about souls.

Every one of us is to be involved in gathering this great harvest of God. When we step out our door each morning, we go into the mission field. Our coworkers and neighbors and family members are the people God has placed us among. Or perhaps the Lord may want us to pack our bags and go to another country. The fields are white for harvest in the world today.

I do not understand the mentality of Christians who are upset about people immigrating to America from different nations and cultures and religions. To me it is a great blessing—the mission field is coming to us. God is bringing people from the Middle East, from Asia, from South America so that we can bring the gospel to them.

The townspeople were touched by the woman's testimony. It piqued their interest in Christ, so they went and listened to Jesus themselves. They told the woman, "We believe now not just because of what you said but because we've heard Him for ourselves. This man really is the Christ, the Savior of the world."

Ultimately, each person is saved by hearing Christ speak to him or her personally, but our testimony may be the tool that the Holy Spirit uses to draw a person to the Savior. Let's ask God to give us opportunities to speak to the people in our world.

 APPLICATION

God wants to use you. The laborer in this story was a simple, sinful woman, but she brought a crowd of people to meet Jesus. If you are scared to witness for Christ, simply pray, "Lord, I am willing. Open a door for me to share Your love with someone today." He can do a great deal with a life that is yielded to Him.

 PRAYER

Lord, thank You that where You have placed us—among our neighbors and coworkers and family members and friends—is not an accident. Open up doors, Lord, and give us boldness. Send us not just across the street but across the country or across the ocean to those who need to hear Your Word. In Jesus' name. Amen.

HEARING AND BELIEVING

Sometimes we receive a promise from God—something He has impressed on our hearts that He will do for us and in us and through us. But then the Lord lets circumstances go in a completely different direction from what we expected, and there we are, totally confused. *Was that really the Lord, or did I just make that up?* we wonder.

Jesus had just returned to Galilee from Judea. In the town of Cana, where He had turned water to wine, a nobleman from Capernaum came to Jesus. Capernaum was a fair distance from Cana, but this man had heard stories of the miracles Jesus had done, and he needed a miracle. He implored the Lord to come and heal his son who was sick. Jesus' response to the nobleman was a bit of a rebuke: "Unless you people see signs and wonders, you will by no means believe" (4:48).

Despite Jesus' rebuke, the man begged Jesus to come with him. But Jesus didn't exactly grant his request. He simply said, "Go your way; your son lives" (4:50). He required from this nobleman an element of faith. Jesus forced the man to take Him at His word. And that's exactly what the man did.

When the nobleman got home, he found things exactly as Jesus had said. Not only was his son healed, but he had become well at the very hour Jesus had told him that his son lived.

This man "believed the word that Jesus spoke to him" (4:50). Our decision to believe or disbelieve what God has said will make all the difference in our lives. If we can't believe what we read in the Bible, we will suffer greatly. The eventual outcome will be tragic, because without faith it is impossible to please God (see Heb. 11:6).

God uses His Word to speak to us personally. When we remain confident in what He has told us, we find peace and security. The nobleman took Jesus at His Word, and I am certain that when he left Jesus, he left confidently. He trusted that Jesus' word was good and that it would be kept.

But sometimes, as we wait for God's Word to be fulfilled, things don't look as if they're going so well. Everything seems black. "Lord, wait!" we say. "I thought You told me this." We become frustrated and anxious. We might even try to accomplish things ourselves rather than wait for God to fulfill His promise, and doing so inevitably makes a mess of things. Of course, even when we have lapses of faith, God keeps His promises to us. But when we allow doubt to invade our thinking, we miss out on the confidence and rest and joy that we could have while we wait for God to fulfill His Word.

Why does God give us promises and then seem to back off and let things go haywire? He is testing our faith. God will let our circumstances go in every which direction until His promises seem impossible to fulfill. And then He'll watch us. "Do you believe Me?" He says. "Didn't I promise you?" God wants to develop character in our lives. He wants us to be people of faith.

There is an interesting contrast throughout the Scriptures between seeing and hearing. We see it in the book of Romans: "Faith comes by hearing and hearing by the Word of God" (Rom. 10:17). Yet we often think that faith comes by seeing. We ought to know better, because a lot of people in the Bible who saw serious miracles, like the parting of the Red Sea, didn't believe. And the masses of people who saw Jesus' miracles didn't follow Him in the end.

The blessing is for those who *hear* and believe. That's how faith develops.

 APPLICATION

 PRAYER

What has God promised you? Even if it seems impossible that it could ever be fulfilled or you wonder whether you heard God correctly—steady yourself. It's certainly possible that we can get things wrong, but it's also highly probable that you got it right. God has His time. He's working out a plan. Trust His Word, and stand on His promises.

Lord, thank You that what You have promised, You will perform. Help us to believe the word that You have spoken to us personally. Make us like this nobleman who took You at Your word. Your prescription for relief from anxiety is that we let our requests be made known to You and then remain confident that You will keep Your promise to us. Strengthen our hearts. In Jesus' name. Amen.

THE PLIGHT OF MAN AND THE POWER OF GOD

Many of us were taught right from wrong at an early age. And we generally believed what we heard. But sometimes we look at the world and think, *That looks so fun! I wish I could do that. But I'm a Christian, so I'm missing out.* Don't be deceived. Sin always produces unhappy results.

Jesus had ministered for a while in Galilee, but now He traveled once again to Jerusalem to attend a feast. As He walked near the temple one day, He passed a pool called Bethesda, around which were several other pools and five covered porches. In this beautiful place multitudes of infirm people lay, hoping to be delivered of their maladies.

Sin has brought a great deal of misery into the world. Blindness, lameness, paralysis, disaster—every harmful or hateful thing has its origin in sin. People often ask, "If God is love, why is there so much trouble in the world?" God created all things good, but man's rebellion against God brought sin into the world, and painful things resulted—war, famine, disease, natural disaster. One day God will remove sin from the world. What a glorious day that will be!

Beside the pool Jesus saw a man who had an infirmity for thirty-eight years. When He saw that the man had been ill for so long, Jesus said to him, "Do you want to be made well?" (5:6).

This man had been forgotten and overlooked in the multitude of sick people. But Jesus noticed him. He saw his plight. Jesus said to the man, "Rise, take up your bed and walk" (5:8). Immediately the man was healed, and he picked up his bed and walked.

Most of us can relate to this man's situation. We may feel neglected or overlooked. But Jesus sees us. He knows the trouble we're in. Jesus never sees one of His people in distress without feeling compassion and offering help.

But here's the interesting thing. Later on Jesus found this man in the temple, and He said to him, "See, you have been made well. Sin no more, lest a worse thing come upon you" (5:14). Every physical infirmity is related to sin, either directly or indirectly, because sickness was a result of sin entering the world. Jesus' warning to this man tells us that his sickness was directly related to sin. In other words, it was sin that had gotten this man into trouble in the first place. For the majority of his life, he had been eaten up by sin.

Sometimes when it seems that God delays in helping us, it's because of sin in our lives. Our trials are not always the direct result of our own sin, of course. But when they are, the only way to deal with the trouble is to deal with the sin—to repent.

What about when our trouble isn't caused directly by sin but simply because we live in a fallen world? Will Jesus deliver us? Jesus chose to heal the man by the pool, but God doesn't heal every physical affliction. However, we can count on the fact that God will take care of us spiritually, which is better. When we are in a state of spiritual well-being, everything else will be put in right order. We can absolutely depend on God for that kind of health.

The plight of man is sin, and the power of God can make us whole. We don't know whether or not God will take away our trials, but He promises us that things will be well with our souls. We can lay hold of that.

 APPLICATION

 PRAYER

The same Jesus who saw that man in his desperate situation sees your need and wants to minister to you. Let Him bring health to your spirit. If you have sin in your life, turn away from it. Repent. It's time to renounce it and say, "Lord, I want to follow You." When Jesus Christ steps into your situation, you can trust Him to take over.

Father, thank You for this wonderful true story of how You met someone through Your Son Jesus Christ and how You care for the helpless. And here we are—in need of Your help. Be present in our lives to touch and heal, forgive and cleanse, deliver and strengthen. In the name of Jesus. Amen.

KNOWING JESUS

It's possible for us to think that we know God when we really don't. Many of the Jewish religious leaders had this problem. So do many today. How do we guard against such deception?

The Lord had just healed a man who had been infirmed for thirty-eight years, which would seem to be cause for rejoicing. But because Jesus had healed this man on the Sabbath, the Jewish leaders, unbelievably, now sought to kill Jesus.

The Jews didn't care that the man had been healed. All they cared about was that Jesus had broken the Sabbath—or rather their tradition regarding the Sabbath. The rabbis considered it fine to *prevent* a person from dying on the Sabbath but not to *promote* healing. According to their rules, Jesus had committed an infraction.

Jesus spoke plainly to the religious leaders: "My Father has been working until now, and I have been working" (5:17). With this statement He added insult to injury. Not only had He "broken" the Sabbath, but now He claimed equality with God. Then Jesus became downright direct: "The Father Himself testifies of Me. But you have never heard the Father's voice" (see John 5:37). The Pharisees, by this time, were undoubtedly irate. They were God's spokesmen, were they not? But Jesus told them that they were under a delusion.

A number of books have come out recently to promote a new type of Christianity. Their authors contrast what they call "old-school believers" and "new-school believers"— old-school believers being judgmental and unloving and new-school believers being wonderful, compassionate, gracious—everything the old-school believers are not. The author of one of these books told a story about a movie he had watched—one full of sex, violence, and vulgarity—and said that God had spoken to him more through that movie than in his past twenty visits to church. The author was proud of this fact. God never speaks to him in church, because that is old school, but God spoke volumes to him through this movie.

My thought, quite honestly, was that this poor guy doesn't know what God's voice sounds like. He was emotionally impacted by the movie, and he mistook his emotional response for the voice of God.

How can we know the difference between our own impressions and the voice of God? How do we make sure that we're not deceiving ourselves, like the Pharisees, thinking that we know God when we don't?

First, of course, everything we hear must be confirmed by the principles and truths in God's Word. But in reading the Bible, we must go beyond its propositions and facts to a personal knowledge of Jesus. Some people focus on Bible doctrine and miss the gospel itself. The Jewish leaders did: "You search the Scriptures," Jesus told them, "for in them you think you have eternal life. But the Scriptures speak of Me, and you are not willing to come to Me and find life" (see John 5:39-40). What an indictment!

These men were Bible experts, but they rejected the very One the Scriptures spoke of. Yes, we must study the Word and know doctrinal truth, but we must never forget that the Scriptures are not an end in themselves—they are the means to the end: knowing Jesus.

Deception is on the move. This new school of Christianity says that we've had too much Bible study—we need to get out now and live the Word. Well, we certainly need to live it. But how can we have too much of God's Word? Jesus said, "Man shall not live by bread alone, but by every word that proceeds from the mouth of God" (Matt. 4:4). How do we guard against deception? Search the Scriptures, which testify of Jesus.

 APPLICATION

 PRAYER

How is your time in the Word? Is it simply a habit, a discipline, an educational experience— or an encounter with Jesus? Reading the Word of God will move us to worship, to obedience, to love, to action, and to proclamation of the good news. If this isn't true for you, ask God to open your heart to the person of Jesus, the living Word, and reveal Him to you in the pages of Scripture.

Thank You, Lord, for the many things we can glean from this discourse You had with the Pharisees. May Your Word work in us, abide in us, and bear much fruit in us. As we give ourselves to the study and meditation of Your Word, which testifies of You, may our experience of You become sweeter and greater, for Your glory. In the name of Jesus. Amen.

LABORING FOR FOOD THAT LASTS

What do you spend most of your time on? Many enjoyable things are legitimate pursuits. But the things that will most satisfy us—and grow the kingdom of God—are those things that will last for eternity.

Jesus crossed the Sea of Galilee, and a great multitude, enamored by His signs, followed Him. When Jesus saw the crowd, He put in motion a plan to show His disciples that nothing is impossible for God. Using only five barley loaves and two fish, Jesus miraculously fed more than five thousand men, plus women and children. He made so much food that the disciples collected twelve baskets of fragments afterward. Amazing!

When the people saw this sign, they said, "This is truly the Prophet who is to come into the world" (6:14). The miracle blew their minds, to put it in modern vernacular. They knew that Jesus had to be the Messiah. They began to strategize how they would promote Him to the throne. Jesus, knowing their intentions, slipped away alone.

As evening approached, the disciples got into the boat and headed back to Capernaum. It was dark, and the sea was rough. Suddenly, as they rowed against the storm, they saw Jesus walking on the water toward them. They were afraid, to say the least. But Jesus called out to them, "It is I; do not be afraid" (6:20).

In this incident in the middle of the chapter, Jesus was teaching His disciples. The miracle He had done had not yet sunk in for them—"they had not understood about the loaves because their hearts were hardened" (Mark 6:52). Jesus wanted these men to know that He was the Lord, the sovereign, all-powerful One, and that they must depend fully on Him. Later, when He would send them out, they would need to know this.

When Jesus arrived on the other side of the sea, the crowd, who had gotten there before Him, cried, "Lord, we've been looking for You! We want to be Your disciples." But Jesus saw through it. "You want to satisfy your physical need, not your spiritual need," He told them. "Don't labor for food that perishes" (see John 6:25-27).

So often people spend their lives focused on things that will eventually perish. We do need to provide for ourselves and our families—the Bible tells us to do this. But God's

Word also tells us that these things shouldn't consume our lives. We must "seek first the kingdom of God" (Matt. 6:33), knowing that God will take care of our needs.

The people asked the Lord, "How do we labor for the kingdom, then?"

Jesus answered, "Believe in the One God has sent."

The people didn't like that. They wanted more bread. They didn't realize that Jesus was trying to give them true bread—Himself. The woman at the well hadn't grasped it at first either. "Give me this water," she'd said, "so I won't have to draw anymore" (see John 4:15).

Jesus spoke again: "I am the bread of life. He who comes to Me shall never hunger, and he who believes in Me shall never thirst" (6:35). This is the first of the seven "I am" statements of Christ found in the gospel of John. When God revealed Himself to Moses, He told Moses that His name is I AM that I AM (see Ex. 3:13-14)—that He is totally self-sufficient. Jesus took that name and seven times added something to it that corresponds to a human need. This first time He said, "I am the bread of life."

With so many pleasures around us, we can forget that we are creatures made in God's image and primarily spiritual beings. We eat, drink, and fulfill our bodily appetites. But Jesus reminds us, "I am the bread. I am the One who brings fulfillment."

Jesus' words did not enhance His popularity. His statements brought Him into direct conflict with the religious leaders in particular. But Jesus was unconcerned with ratings. He came to offer the Bread of Life so that men and women might find eternal satisfaction in Him.

 APPLICATION

 PRAYER

Are you trying to satisfy your soul with food that perishes? Jesus is the Bread of Life. He is the only possibility for finding satisfaction. Don't resist Him. Don't oppose Him. Let go of temporary things and ask God to increase Your love for the things of His kingdom.

Father, help us to rise above the material world that we live in. You created this world for us to enjoy, but You called us to be Your servants while we live here. Help us to seek the things that endure for eternity. In Jesus' name. Amen.

THE LIVING BREAD FROM HEAVEN

In His teaching Jesus sometimes used startling terminology. With His difficult statements He blew apart people's preconceived notions and conveyed spiritual realities. Let's be glad that He did! In doing so Jesus showed us the way to salvation.

The conversation that began between Jesus and the Jews, when the people tried to make Jesus king, took place over several days. It began on the shore of the Galilee and culminated in the synagogue. Jesus would speak; the Jews would then respond and go away to discuss it. It was an ongoing debate.

Jesus told these men, among other things, that He was the Bread of Life. The Jews, who sought fulfillment by other means, became offended.

Jesus knew that the Jews were complaining, "What's He talking about, saying He came down from heaven? Isn't this Jesus? We know His father and mother." His reply to them was significant: "Do not murmur among yourselves. No one can come to Me unless the Father who sent Me draws him" (6:43-44).

This statement needs to be understood. Jesus was reminding the Jews that salvation is ultimately of the Lord—not of the Jewish religious system itself. These religious leaders appeared to be in tune with God, but Jesus told them, "You don't know God. You're murmuring about Me because you're not being drawn by the Father."

Despite the Jews' displeasure, Jesus reiterated His claim: "I am the living bread which came down from heaven" (6:51). Jesus didn't change His message because the Jews didn't like it. He made His point again.

People get upset with Christians today. *Don't say that Jesus is the only way to God!* they say. How should we respond? By repeating the message. It's the truth. We should never back down from the truth.

Jesus not only refused to withdraw His claim, He now used offensive terminology to expound on it: "Unless you eat the flesh of the Son of Man and drink His blood, you have no life in you" (6:53). This statement was highly abhorrent to His listeners. It was strictly forbidden under the Mosaic system to drink blood.

In saying these things Jesus was sifting the wheat from the chaff. He was separating those who were interested in Him for wrong reasons from those whose motives were right. We are into big numbers. We judge a meeting's validity by the number of people who show up. Jesus didn't have a numbers hang-up. In fact, His words were so offensive to those following Him that many decided they couldn't handle what He had to say and left.

What exactly did Jesus mean by saying that His followers were to eat His flesh and drink His blood? The Roman Catholic Church has concluded that Jesus gives us His actual body and blood when we take Communion. But Scripture offers no support for this idea. Later, when Jesus distributed the bread and the cup to His disciples, how could the bread have been His physical body? His body was fully intact as He broke the bread. And He referred to the cup as the "fruit of the vine" (Matt. 26:29)—actual wine. Clearest of all is that when Jesus made His statement to the crowd, He used the aorist verb tense, which expresses a one-time event, not a repeated event like Communion.

So what was this one-time event He spoke of? Receiving Him. We receive Christ not through the partaking of a sacrament but by putting our faith in Jesus Christ. In this one-time event of receiving Christ, we fulfill Jesus' command to eat His flesh and drink His blood.

The religious leaders were offended by these words, but we can be unspeakably thankful that Jesus spoke them. The gospel offends the natural man, but in doing so it leads us to life. May we receive Jesus, the Bread of Life, and continue to grow in Him by feeding on His Word.

 APPLICATION

 PRAYER

Have you partaken of Jesus, the Bread of Life? If you haven't, will you receive Him today? If you have, are you feasting on the Word of God? Spend as much time in the Word of God as you can. In Jesus' words we will find supernatural power, and our spiritual man will be edified.

Lord, thank You that Your words are spirit and life. Help us, Lord, to feed upon You, the living bread, and to feed upon Your Word consistently. You alone have the words of eternal life. Increase Your life in us, we pray. In the name of Jesus. Amen.

TO WHOM SHALL WE GO?

Quite often those of us who claim to be servants of Christ are reluctant to say hard things. Some believers even take a position in which they refuse to do so. But this is a total contradiction of Scripture.

Jesus said many hard things. As He finished speaking to the Jews about partaking of His body and blood, many of those who followed Jesus complained about His teaching. "This is a hard teaching," they said. "Who can understand it?" (6:60). Jesus wasn't out to win a popularity contest. He was interested in the truth rather than in what people wanted to hear.

Some Christian leaders today refuse to talk about sin or hell. Others won't use the word "saved" in case they make an unsaved person feel badly. But when we take these positions, we disregard the example of Jesus.

Jesus went out of His way to say things that unsettled people. He could have told the Jews, "Let me explain what I mean by eating My flesh and drinking My blood. I don't mean it literally." But He didn't. He wanted the seriousness of the matter to be driven home to His listeners.

The great sin of this century is offending somebody. The problem with this perspective, though, is that it comes from people thinking completely in the realm of the flesh. Jesus told the Jews, "the flesh profits nothing" (6:63). It is the spirit of man that goes on living forever, either in heaven or in hell. We have an obligation to the realm of the spirit. If we think in terms of the flesh, we will inevitably fail in our task to reach people with the gospel.

Here is the reality: the gospel is an offense. The apostles came along preaching the gospel and penning the New Testament, and in so doing they directly opposed the Roman system, since Caesar had usurped the place of God. Of course, Peter and Paul and the other disciples were in trouble most of the time. But if we try to avoid offense in preaching the gospel, inevitably we will have to deny the message itself. We should rather be persecuted than deny the gospel of Jesus Christ.

We don't want to offend people unnecessarily, of course. We're not to go out and arrogantly tell people, "Hey, you're wrong. Your lifestyle will bring judgment upon you." The Bible tells us, "Always be ready to give a defense to everyone who asks you a reason for the hope that is in you, with meekness and fear [respect]" (1 Pet. 3:15). We need to deliver the message in love, although the message, even given in love, quite often will offend.

There is not a sadder verse in the entire Bible than this: "From that time many of His disciples went back and walked with Him no more" (6:66). Many of Jesus' disciples could not endure what He was saying.

"Then Jesus said to the twelve, 'Do you also want to go away?' But Simon Peter answered Him, 'Lord, to whom shall we go? You [and You alone] have the words of eternal life'" (6:67–68). That was the right answer, Peter. And it's true for us. Where could we possibly go? Where else can we find forgiveness of sins? Where else can we receive eternal life? Nowhere.

Peter summed up his conclusion: "We have come to believe and know that You are the Christ, the Son of the living God" (6:69). Jesus' sayings are hard, but He alone has the words of eternal life. The biggest favor we could do for anybody is to speak the truth in love, not holding back the message of the gospel.

 APPLICATION

 PRAYER

Are you afraid to speak the truth when it may offend or anger someone? We must never be rude or arrogant or prideful, but we must never be afraid, even if it causes some to be offended. Our allegiance must be to Jesus first and foremost, beyond even our family ties, beyond our closest friends. Eternity is at stake.

Lord, thank You that You gave Yourself for us. It's a small thing for You to ask us to give ourselves to You in return. We have no life except the one that You've given us. Help us, Lord, to share the truth with others in love. We pray in Jesus' name and for His glory and honor. Amen.

IF ANYONE THIRSTS

Sometimes in our Christian life we become dry and unfruitful. But Jesus intends that we be filled to overflowing with His water of life. Do you need refreshing?

Because the leadership in Judea was plotting to kill Him, Jesus had steered clear of Jerusalem for about six months and ministered in Galilee. The Feast of Tabernacles, however, was about to take place, and Jesus' brothers, who still didn't believe in Him, pressed Him to go to it. "My time has not yet come" (7:6), Jesus calmly replied.

At the Feast of Tabernacles, the Jews praised God for the completion of the harvest. They also built booths, little tabernacles, and lived in them for a week, remembering God's faithfulness to their ancestors during their journey to the Promised Land.

After the feast began, Jesus went to it, "not openly, but as it were in secret" (7:10). All over Jerusalem He was the topic of conversation and controversy. As Jesus began to teach, people puzzled over Him: "Isn't this the Man the leaders want to kill? Why aren't they taking Him in? Maybe they've decided that He's the Messiah after all." But many believed in Him. "He's got to be the Messiah," they said.

By Jesus' time, a spectacular ritual had developed around the Feast of Tabernacles. Each day of the feast, the priests walked in a procession to the pool of Siloam and filled pitchers with water. Then they climbed the temple stairs to the altar and there, on the stone steps, poured out the water. This was reminiscent of water coming forth from the rock when the Israelites had wandered in the wilderness.

Now, on the final day of the feast, the priest dramatically poured the water on the stone. The people were gathered in a festive mood, and Jesus, almost certainly at the feast's climactic moment, stood, probably in the very place where the priest had poured out the water, and cried out, "If anyone thirsts, let him come to Me and drink" (7:37).

Jesus, of course, was not offering literal water. He was appealing to the spiritual thirst in people's hearts. He was calling people to satisfy their thirst in Him. He was not calling people to religion, which is what the Jewish leaders offered, or to church—although hopefully we can find Jesus at church—or to good works. He was calling people to Himself. Jesus' invitation is about a relationship with God.

Jesus continued, "He who believes in Me, as the Scripture has said, out of his heart will flow rivers of living water" (7:38). The prophet Ezekiel writes about a river that will flow one day from the throne of God in the millennial kingdom, "and everything will live wherever the river goes" (Ezek. 47:9). Jesus was saying that a river of life will proceed from all those who believe in Him and will bring life to everyone it touches. In other words, salvation is not just for our own personal benefit—it is to gush forth from us and touch the lives of others.

Jesus was speaking of the Holy Spirit, whom He would send after His death and resurrection. That day has now come. As Christ is enthroned in our lives, the Holy Spirit lives within us, and His power flows from us and brings life wherever it goes. It is powerful and glorious.

Many who heard Jesus said, "'Truly this is the Prophet.' Others said, 'This is the Christ'" (7:40–41). The officers who had been sent to arrest Jesus returned to the religious leaders empty-handed. The leaders demanded, "Where is He?" and the officers responded, "No man ever spoke like this Man!" (7:46). So the debate continued between those who were willing to hear and those who refused.

May the river of living water that Jesus promised us indeed flow from us and into the lives of others.

 APPLICATION

 PRAYER

Are you barren and dry and dying for lack of water in any area of your life? Will you hear Jesus' invitation to come to Him and drink? When the Lord pours His water of life upon you, you will be refreshed and revived. Then spiritual prosperity will come forth from you and refresh others.

Lord, may the river of Your Holy Spirit flow into our lives and our fellowships so that we may be revitalized and Your life be imparted to those around us. Lord, we are thirsty for You. Fill us up, we pray. In Jesus' name. Amen.

JESUS, FRIEND OF SINNERS

All of us know that horrible moment of being caught in some sin. The consequences of it can be humiliating and shameful. How does God deal with us when we fail?

After the Feast of Tabernacles, hundreds of thousands of people remained in Jerusalem. Jesus was at the temple area early the next morning, teaching again, when suddenly a group of scribes and Pharisees burst into the crowd, dragging a woman. The Jews cast her before Jesus and said, "We caught this woman in the act of adultery. The Law says she should be stoned—what do You say?" (see John 8:4-5).

Of course, we have to wonder, *Where was the man?* The religious leaders clearly had no concern for righteousness. This scenario was intended to trap Jesus: If He pardoned the woman, He would violate the law of Moses. If He condemned her, He would subject Himself to Roman judgment, since the Romans prohibited the Jews from carrying out capital punishment.

Jesus calmly acted as though the religious leaders were not there. He stooped down and began to write in the dirt with His finger. Bible teachers have guessed at what Jesus wrote, but I would speculate that Jesus was writing the Ten Commandments in the dirt, just as God did when He wrote with His finger on tablets of stone.

When the leaders pressured Jesus for an answer, He said to them, "He who is without sin among you, let him throw a stone at her first" (8:7). If Jesus did write the Ten Commandments, the religious leaders were faced with them all. As they looked at them, each and every one came under conviction. The oldest among the group, who were probably the wisest, left first. One by one, they all departed.

Jesus said to the woman, "Woman, where are those accusers of yours? Has no one condemned you?" (8:10). The term "woman" that Jesus used here is a gentle one. Imagine the contrast between Jesus and these men, who had literally dragged the woman out of an adulterous situation and thrown her at Jesus' feet. "No one, Lord," the woman replied, and Jesus said to her, "Neither do I condemn you" (8:11).

Jesus, interestingly, being the only sinless One in the bunch, was the only One qualified to stone the woman. But this One, who could have justifiably cast stones at the woman, said, "Neither do I condemn you." As representatives of Jesus, our first approach to people should always be to draw them in through the love of God. To do this, we must keep in mind the fact that we too are sinners saved by grace.

In forgiving the woman, the Lord didn't gloss over her sin. Before she left He told her, "Go and sin no more" (8:11). He didn't say, "Hey, don't worry about it—no problem." God is full of grace; He receives sinners. But He receives us in order to deliver us from the power of sin. Regarding our past sins, He tells us, "I don't condemn you—I forgive you. But as far as the future goes, go and sin no more."

In our day, the message that Jesus came to save us from the power of sin is being replaced with all kinds of philosophy and psychology. Subsequently, we have so much compromise in the church. But Jesus said, "Go and sin no more." And His command brings with it the power for us to obey.

We all sin to some degree. But while for the unbeliever sin is the rule, for the believer, sin is the exception. When we come to Christ, the power of sin is broken. We may stumble into sin because of weakness, but we don't live consistently in sin any longer.

 APPLICATION

 PRAYER

When we come to Jesus having sinned, His heart toward us is one of compassion. But never forget that in His forgiveness, there is with it the command to go and sin no more—and the power for us to do it. If you struggle to lay down some area of sin in your life, receive Jesus' grace toward you, then take courage, deliberately lay aside your sin, and return to it no more.

Thank You, Lord, for this wonderful account of Your dealings with this woman, who could have justifiably been stoned. You showed Your heart of compassion and Your longing to forgive sins. But Lord, You also showed that having been forgiven, we are to go and sin no more. Thank You, Jesus, that we are no longer slaves of sin. In Jesus' name. Amen.

THE TRUTH SHALL MAKE YOU FREE

At times we feel oppressed by some mental block. Maybe the Devil has lied to you, saying something like, *Did you see how that person at church looked at you? He doesn't like you. You shouldn't go back there.* Then the truth comes in. Somebody comes up and says, *So-and-so was just telling me what a wonderful brother you are. He's so glad you're part of the church.* Immediately, you're set free. That's what the truth does for us.

As He finished speaking to the woman caught in adultery, Jesus told the crowd, "I am the light of the world. He who follows Me shall not walk in darkness, but have the light of life" (8:12). This is Jesus' second "I am" statement. The tragedy is that as Jesus declared this facet of who He was, He was once again met with resistance from the Pharisees.

Despite their rejection of Him, Jesus kept pleading with them. As the large, mixed crowd around Him observed another prolonged dispute develop between Jesus and the religious leaders, some of them realized, "This guy Jesus knows what He's talking about—these other guys don't have a clue." At this they believed in Jesus.

Jesus seemed to direct His words at this point more to these Jews who believed in Him than to the leaders: "If you abide in My word, you are My disciples indeed. And you shall know the truth, and the truth shall make you free" (8:31–32). Those of us who believe in Jesus today need to hear this as well.

The great tragedy in the church is its neglect of the Word of God. Throughout church history, whenever the Word of God has been exalted, proclaimed, and believed, the church has prospered and been effective. Whenever God's Word has been neglected and disbelieved, the church has plunged into catastrophe and ineffectiveness.

Today even the Evangelical Church is in some quarters rejecting the Bible and embracing seeker-sensitive and Emerging Church movements. These groups are diminishing the significance of God's Word, rejecting its authority and sufficiency. But Christians cannot live victoriously when disconnected from the Word of God.

The word "abide" could be translated "continue" or "stay." Its implication is "live." When the Word of God becomes as important to us as our daily bread, then we're living in it. And we're Jesus' disciples indeed.

When we abide in the Word, we will know the truth, and the truth will make us free. But many Christians are in bondage to sin. Does the gospel not work? No, Christians are in bondage because they do not abide in the Word. They come to Christ and are set free. But they fail to go deeper in the Word, and problems creep back into their lives. Some even end up in gross, blatant sin.

To abide in the Word implies obedience to the Word. But to obey the Word, we've got to know it. We've got to spend time in it. As we grow in our knowledge of what God says, we will be able to obey Him.

"Word" in English comes from several different Greek words. The Greek word *rhema* means "a specific word." A rhema is what you receive when you open up the Scripture, and right there is God's word to you for your specific situation. God wants to give us those words—to show us the truth, to set us free—as we abide in His Word.

The world is under massive deception, and it's getting worse. Rapidly. At a certain point the Devil will incarnate himself in a man and say, "I am God," and everybody will believe it. With all the lies swirling around us today, we must know the truth. We must abide in the Word. Then we will truly be Jesus' disciples. We will know the truth, and the truth will make us free.

 ## APPLICATION

 ## PRAYER

Are you walking in freedom or tangled up by some lie? If you're not free, it's because you are either unaware of the truth or not obeying the truth. Decide today to get into the Word and receive the truth. Then act upon it—and experience the freedom that Christ came to bring.

Lord, how we appreciate that You came to set us free from our bondage to sin. Yet at times we still become entangled in sin by believing a lie of some sort. Lord, help us to live in the truth of Your Word so that we can walk in Your freedom. We pray in Jesus' name. Amen.

MURDER, LIES, AND THE DEVIL

The Devil attacks people. He tells us things like, "You're fat. You're ugly. Everybody hates you. You ought to kill yourself. Don't go back to that church." So many of the maladies that people suffer in our culture are rooted in Satan's deception and lies.

Jesus was disputing with the Pharisees before a large crowd. Although these men had persistently rejected Jesus, the Lord had been patient and long-suffering toward them. Now Jesus was about to get pretty rough with the religious leaders. "If God were your Father," He told them, "you would love Me. You are of your father the devil, because you want to do the things he does" (see 8:42–44). This obviously provoked the Jews to anger.

What are the desires of the Devil that Jesus accused the Pharisees of having toward Him? First, the Devil is a murderer. Wherever we see murderous activity, we can know that the Devil is behind it. Second, the Devil is a liar. "When he speaks a lie, he speaks from his own resources, for he is a liar and the father of it" (8:44). Jesus knew that in their hearts, the religious leaders wanted to destroy and kill Him.

Throughout history, the Devil has inspired men to murder, deception, and falsehood. As Christians, we should never forget this, because the Devil works overtime to try to infiltrate the church with the same deceptive philosophies by which he has duped the world. There is so little proof of any validity to the theory of evolution, yet Christians come along and say, "The church has historically opposed progress and science, and we don't want to be a bunch of old-fashioned dummies." That's an infiltration of satanic philosophy into the church.

The Devil attacks people personally, as well. Young girls who are afflicted with anorexia or bulimia weigh ninety pounds, yet think, *I'm fat.* Psychologists and philosophers have all kinds of theories about what's going on. I'll tell you: the Devil is deceiving people.

Jesus continued to lay into the religious leaders: "He who is of God hears God's words; therefore you do not hear, because you are not of God" (8:47). There comes a time when we have to go toe-to-toe with people. Yes, we need to be loving and compassionate, but we cannot withhold truth. Sometimes we have to let the chips fall where they may.

Proponents of the Emerging Church movement say that one of the virtues of a Christian leader is to have more questions than answers. The world loves this. "Here's a guy we can get behind," they say. "He's vulnerable. He's just like the next guy, struggling along, hoping he has it right." That is the antithesis of what Jesus was like. Jesus spoke with authority. His servants ought to speak with authority as well.

Jesus wound up the conversation with a bang: "You don't know My Father, but I do. If I said I didn't know Him, I'd be a liar, just as you are." He didn't pull any punches. "You may not receive Me, but your father Abraham rejoiced to see My day."

The Pharisees shot back with hostility, "You're not even fifty years old, and You've seen Abraham?"

Jesus emphatically declared, "Before Abraham was, I AM" (8:58). Jesus was not simply claiming to have preexisted. By taking to Himself the name by which God had revealed Himself to Moses: I AM that I AM (see Ex. 3:14), He was claiming to be God. The Jews knew it, and they wanted to kill Him for blasphemy.

We live in a world that hated Jesus and will, to a large degree, hate us too. Let's be proud to stand for God in this wicked and perverse generation. May we gain discernment into the activity of the Devil so that he will not deceive us.

 APPLICATION

If you have been tormented with thoughts of worthlessness, thoughts that nobody loves you, that God doesn't love you, that God has condemned or wants to destroy you or can't save you, this is not the voice of the Lord. Resist these lies of the Devil and receive deliverance as you put your trust in God's Word.

 PRAYER

Lord, we are blessed to stand for You in this wicked and perverse generation. Give us discernment into the activity of the Devil, and keep us from being deceived by him. Deliver us from thoughts that torment our minds, and help us to put our trust in Your Word. You are the great I AM. We pray in Your name. Amen.

I ONCE WAS BLIND, BUT NOW I SEE

Have you experienced a personal touch from God in some area of your life? When the Lord delivers us personally, it is pretty convincing proof to our hearts of His kindness and grace. Despite obvious proofs, however, some people refuse to believe in God.

Jesus' disciples, having been taught by the Jewish religious system that disease was the direct result of the afflicted person's sin, were curious when they saw a man who had been born blind: Was it the man who had sinned, they asked Jesus, or his parents?

Jesus cleared things up quickly: neither. God had allowed the man to be born blind in order to demonstrate His power in the man's life. Upon finishing this explanation, Jesus "spat on the ground and made clay with the saliva; and He anointed the eyes of the blind man with the clay. And He said to him, 'Go, wash in the pool of Siloam'" (9:6-7). The man did as Jesus told him, and he came back seeing.

The problem with this, at least for the religious leaders, is that once again Jesus had "broken" the Sabbath. When Jesus kneaded mud to form clay, the Pharisees, absurdly, considered His actions a violation of the Law.

The religious leaders questioned the blind man as to how he had been healed. Not content with his straightforward explanation, they called in his parents. "We have no idea how he can now see," his parents answered. "He is of age; ask him" (9:21). They were afraid to say more, since the religious leaders had by this time threatened excommunication for anyone who confessed Jesus as the Messiah.

The Jewish leaders became angry and said to the blind man, "Give God the glory! We know that this Man is a sinner" (9:24). This man had been a beggar all of his adult life, but now he was prepared to stand up to these religious leaders. "Whether He is a sinner or not I do not know," the man answered. "One thing I know: that though I was blind, now I see" (9:25).

Besides being a bold challenge to the Jews, the man's testimony was profound. God had done an obvious work in his life, and that was enough for him. But the Jews continued to press the man. Despite their demands, the truth was crystal clear to him. "Really?" he told the leaders. "You don't know where this Man comes from? He is obviously from God, or He couldn't have done this."

Now the Jews showed their true colors. "You were born in sin, and you dare to teach us?" they cried. And they threw him out of the synagogue. What the man's parents had feared came upon their son.

When Jesus heard of this, He found the man and said to him, "Do you believe in the Son of God?" (9:35). This man looked at Jesus for the first time, hearing again the voice that had told him to go and wash. As he realized who Jesus was, the man cried, "Lord, I believe!"

Jesus came to open the eyes of those who are blind. The person who acknowledges his blindness and sin and cries to God for mercy finds sight.

Jesus also came to pronounce judgment—to close the eyes of those who say they see. The Pharisees thought they had spiritual sight. But before them was God Himself in human flesh, who had just done what no man could do, and they fought against Him from every angle imaginable. The Pharisees' insistence that they were right would eventually bring them to the place where there was no help for them.

Jesus wants to touch us and open our eyes and hearts to the work of His Spirit. Our part is simply to yield to Him.

 APPLICATION

How has God's touch on your life convinced you of His reality and love? Like the blind man, your simple testimony can reveal to others His goodness and grace. Some will refuse to believe, but your proclamation of God's goodness in your life will demonstrate His power to the world around you.

 PRAYER

Thank You, Lord, for Your love and compassion. Where we have blind spots in our lives, help us to humble ourselves before You so that You can give us clear vision. And Lord, give us eyes to see the blind and the lame and the maimed—those to whom You want us to extend Your mercy. In Jesus' name. Amen.

MY SHEEP HEAR MY VOICE

The enemy is crafty. He disguises himself as a caring shepherd in order to gain access into our lives and, ultimately, to destroy us. If we are truly following Jesus, we will sense the enemy's designs and ignore his voice.

Jesus, in His ongoing dialogue with the contradictory Pharisees, told a parable: "He who does not enter the sheepfold by the door, but climbs up some other way, the same is a thief and a robber. But he who enters by the door is the shepherd of the sheep" (10:1-2). This was a direct indictment against the Jewish leaders. Jesus was calling these men, who claimed to be shepherds of Israel, thieves and robbers. The Pharisees' animosity toward Jesus made manifest that they were not truly God's servants.

What do thieves do? Steal, kill, and destroy. The Pharisees had taken the system that Moses had passed on to them and ripped the heart out of it, replacing it with their humanistic thoughts and ideas. In misrepresenting the law of Moses, they were depriving people of salvation.

The religious leaders did not understand Jesus' illustration. "I am the door of the sheep," He explained. "If anyone enters by Me, he will be saved" (10:7, 9). This is the third "I am" statement made by Jesus. He is the door, the only One through whom a person can enter the sheepfold—the kingdom of God. In contrast to the leaders, who seemed unconcerned with people's salvation, Jesus said, "I have come that they may have life, and that they may have it more abundantly" (10:10).

Jesus quickly followed His third "I am" statement with a fourth: "I am the good shepherd" (10:11). The term "good shepherd" often reminds us of Psalm 23. But hundreds of years before Jesus came to earth, the Lord expressed a complaint against the leaders of Israel in the book of Ezekiel:

> "Woe to the shepherds of Israel who feed themselves! Should not the shepherds feed the flocks? I will establish one shepherd over them, and he shall feed them—My servant David. He shall feed them and be their

shepherd. And I, the LORD, will be their God, and My servant David a
prince among them; I, the LORD, have spoken" (Ezek. 34:2, 23-24).

When Jesus told the Pharisees, "I am the Good Shepherd," I have a feeling that they thought of Ezekiel 34. Jesus Himself was the "one shepherd" that God was establishing over Israel to care for them. No wonder the Jews were jealous of Him.

Jesus made a further distinction between Himself and the religious leaders: "I am the Good Shepherd, and I demonstrate it by laying down My life for the sheep. A hireling won't do that." The religious leaders were hirelings. They did their job for prestige and power—everything except for the people.

Sheep are tuned in to their shepherd's voice. If another person calls them, even if he imitates the shepherd's voice exactly, the sheep will not respond. Among the common people of Israel there was obviously a growing dissatisfaction regarding their spiritual leaders, because many were forsaking the Pharisees and following Jesus. Jesus was the true Shepherd, and the people knew His voice.

When the Lord speaks to us, even though at times He rebukes or challenges us, there is love in His voice. Like sheep, we won't listen to anyone else. What was it that tuned the sheep to the shepherd's voice? The sense of their shepherd's love and concern for them.

The Lord's voice comforts—it reminds us that we are His and He is ours. May our hearts be tender and our ears be tuned to the voice of our Shepherd.

 APPLICATION

 PRAYER

Do you ever listen to voices of condemnation and heaviness and guilt? "I think the Lord is angry with me," you say. "I don't even know if I'll make it to heaven." That's not the voice of the Good Shepherd. It's the voice of the Devil, the accuser of the brethren. Run to the true Shepherd, Jesus Christ. His voice will calm and comfort and strengthen your heart.

Thank You, Jesus, that You are the door, the way to the Father, and that You are the Good Shepherd. You love us, and You laid down Your life for us—the greatest demonstration of love. In any area of our lives in which the thief has robbed us or is trying to kill or destroy us, Lord, we pray that You will grant us Your abundant life. In Jesus' name. Amen.

TRYING TO KILL GOD

Jesus fed people, healed the sick, even raised the dead. He did many good works. Why is it, then, that the Jews did not believe in Him—in fact, were downright hostile toward Him? For that matter, why are so many in our day combative when it comes to Jesus?

As Jesus walked one day through Solomon's porch, where rabbis often gathered to lecture their students, the Jews said to Him, "How long do You keep us in doubt? If You are the Christ, tell us plainly" (10:24). Jesus quite clearly met every scriptural criteria for the Messiah. He had also claimed on numerous occasions that He was indeed the promised Deliverer. The problem with the Jews' unbelief was not a lack of evidence but a refusal to believe.

Jesus pointed this out. "You do not believe, because you are not of My sheep" (10:26). Why were they not His sheep? Jesus had appealed to them many times over. God hadn't predetermined these people's condemnation. They were not His sheep simply because they would not heed His Word.

Jesus clarified, "My sheep hear My voice, and I know them, and they follow Me. No one is able to snatch them out of My Father's hand. I and My Father are one" (10:27, 29–30). At this the Jews took up stones to stone Him—the second time they had attempted to do so (see John 8:58–59). Jesus responded, "I have done many good works from My Father. For which of these do you stone Me?"

We could ask people the same question today: "What exactly has Jesus done that's got you so upset?" Humanists in our culture want to ban Jesus from the public arena. "That cross there on the hillside, it's got to come down," they say. "That nativity scene—we need to get rid of it." The problem, really, is that human nature is set in a position of enmity against God.

The Jews answered, "We don't stone You for good works but because You claim to be God." The Jews understood that Jesus was claiming deity. They wouldn't have picked up stones to throw at Him otherwise.

Over the months Jesus had done many things that the Jewish leaders themselves believed only God could do. The Jews knew the prophecies about the lame leaping for joy, the dumb speaking, the deaf hearing, and the blind seeing (see Isa. 35:5-6). They knew that these miracles were the work of God—and the mark of the messianic kingdom.

"Look," Jesus finally told the Jews, "if it's just too hard for you to receive what I'm saying, since I'm a Galilean, a peasant, not educated in your system, then at least believe the works." But the Jews were incensed. They sought to seize Him.

Despite the leaders' continued resistance, many of the common people looked at the situation rationally. As they observed what Jesus said and did and, no doubt, heard Him debate the Jews, they said, "This has got to be the Messiah." Another gospel tells us, "the common people heard Him gladly" (Mark 12:37).

Many today, like these people, will hear the Lord gladly. But others, no matter how much evidence they see, have already made up their minds to resist. Why? Well, Jesus said it: "You are not My sheep."

In this conversation Jesus extended His gracious invitation to the Jews, in a sense, one last time. After this He left Jerusalem, and He wouldn't return until His final week of ministry. It appears that His striving with the Jewish leaders had ended. Just as in the time of Noah, when God said that His "Spirit shall not strive with man forever" (Gen. 6:3), a person can resist God to the point of no return. And even God Himself cannot help a person who arrives at that point.

 APPLICATION

Antagonism toward Jesus is a strong apologetic that He is somebody significant. No one exerts hostility toward something that isn't a real threat. This bolsters our faith. When you are faced with opposition for the sake of the gospel, take courage. Ask the Lord to strengthen and steady you in your faith, and be fervent in prayer for those who resist the love of Christ.

 PRAYER

Lord, it's hard for us to imagine anyone being filled with animosity toward You. We pray that in these days You will continue to draw people to Yourself. How we thank You, Lord, that we are Your sheep and that no one can snatch us from the Father's hand. In Jesus' name. Amen.

THE RESURRECTION AND THE LIFE

Death comes to all of us. Young and old, rich and poor, good and bad, educated and ignorant, king and commoner. But it's not something we should fear. In fact, Jesus wants us to live boldly for Him in the face of death.

When Jesus received a message that His friend Lazarus, who lived near Jerusalem, was sick and dying, He waited a couple days and then decided to go back to Judea. His disciples reminded Him that the Jews there wanted to kill Him, but Jesus essentially told them, "Don't worry—it's still day. I've got some time left."

When Jesus and His disciples arrived in the village of Bethany, Lazarus had been in the tomb for four days. Martha came to meet Jesus as He approached. "Lord," she said, "if You had been here, my brother would not have died" (11:21). Martha was disappointed. Jesus had come too late.

Jesus sought to reassure her. "Your brother will rise again" (11:23). Martha believed in the resurrection, but at the moment she saw only the immediate circumstance. She replied, in essence, "Lord, I know that he will rise again at the last day—but that doesn't help me right now."

Jesus responded to Martha with the most profound statement He ever uttered: "I am the resurrection and the life. He who believes in Me, though he may die, he shall live. And whoever lives and believes in Me shall never die" (11:25-26).

In this fifth "I am" statement, Jesus, adding to the name "I AM" (meaning, whatever man is in need of), told Martha that He is the victor over death. Jesus was addressing Martha's immediate situation, but He was also promising that anyone who believes in Him will rise again at the last day (see Dan. 12:2; Isa. 26:19).

How do we understand this in light of Jesus' next words to Martha: "Whoever lives and believes in Me shall never die" (11:26)? For a believer in Jesus Christ, what we commonly call death is actually sleep. Our bodies go to sleep, but our spirits rise immediately to be with the Lord. The person who lives and believes in Jesus does not die.

But Martha and Mary's hearts were broken. Mary came out to meet Jesus and said exactly what her sister had said moments earlier: "Lord, if You had been here, my brother would not have died" (11:32). When Jesus saw her weeping, He groaned in His spirit and began to weep.

Why did Jesus weep? He knew that Lazarus was only sleeping—and He was about to remedy that. The Lord was grieved because of the agony that people go through over death. At Lazarus's tomb, Jesus stood face-to-face with the horrific consequences of man's rebellion, and He was deeply troubled over it.

Jesus, groaning again, approached the cave in which Lazarus was buried. "Take away the stone" (11:39), He commanded.

Martha wasn't so sure. "Lord, by this time there is a stench, for he has been dead four days" (11:39). Martha had told Jesus that she believed in the resurrection, but her belief was not perfect. It was like that of the man who had cried out, "Lord, I believe; help my unbelief!" (Mark 9:24).

Jesus prayed aloud and then cried out in a loud voice, "Lazarus, come forth!" (11:43). Lazarus, wrapped in strips of cloth, came out of the tomb.

A lot of us aren't sure that we'll be able to handle death. We'll handle it. Spurgeon said it best: "We don't have dying grace until it's time to die."[3] We need to think about death in biblical terms: to be absent from the body is to be present with the Lord (see 2 Cor. 5:8). What Jesus said to Martha He says to us: "If you live and believe in Me, you will never die. Do you believe this?"

 APPLICATION

The early Christians were successful in getting the gospel to the world. How? One answer is that they were fearless. They weren't afraid to die. Those who have made the greatest impact for the kingdom of God are those who have said, "If they kill me, it's no problem because I'll go to heaven." Let's take the Lord at His Word: "He who believes in Me, though he may die, he shall live."

 PRAYER

Thank You, Lord, that You are the resurrection and the life. Because of that, we will never die. May we live fearlessly for You until You come, completely freed up to boldly share the gospel, not fearing anything but You. We praise You. In Jesus' name. Amen.

LOSING WHAT YOU TRY TO KEEP

We all highly value certain things, some of them legitimate—family, home, friends—and others, like pride or resentment, are dangerous. Either way, when we hold on to something tightly for our own gain, even if it's a good thing, Jesus says that we will eventually lose it.

It's hard to imagine that anybody could witness Jesus raise a man who had been dead for four days and still not believe in Him. But some of those who watched Jesus raise Lazarus reported His actions to the religious leaders. They knew that the Jews were looking for some basis on which to get rid of Jesus.

The Pharisees and the Sadducees, the two groups that made up Israel's religious leaders, weren't on the best of terms. The Sadducees were extremely liberal, while the Pharisees were taken up with every detail of the Law. But the two groups had a common enemy that united them: Jesus of Nazareth.

These factions came together to devise a plan to deal with Jesus Christ. "What shall we do?" they said. "This Man works many signs." The obvious conclusion for a person to draw, upon hearing that Jesus had raised a man from the dead, was that Jesus had to be the Messiah. But these men were concerned about something else: "If we let Him keep doing this, everyone will believe in Him, and the Romans will take away our place and our nation." The Jewish leaders were driven by one thing: keeping their position.

As the leaders debated, Caiaphas, the high priest, interrupted. "Listen," he argued. "It makes more sense that one Man die for the people than that the whole nation perish." Caiaphas, an evil man who would later have Jesus arrested and sentenced to death, was prophesying, although he didn't know it. Caiaphas's words lined up exactly with what the prophets had said the Messiah would do: He would die so that Israel—and the whole world—would not perish. This is the gospel.

Tell me, why are people so up in arms about the gospel? The fact that somebody was punished in our place so that we don't have to perish is good news! The bottom line, in the end, is that people do not want to be told what to do. They want to maintain their autonomy.

This perspective is driving our culture today. As in Jesus' day, when the Jews decided to get rid of the Lord to save their own position, people wanted to get rid of Jesus in order to maintain their independence. We see it in the uproar over the use of the term "Christmas." We see it in the reaction to Christian prayer in any public arena and in the secularization of our educational system. Atheists and unbelievers don't want this entity called the church telling them that God requires them to live a certain way. Ultimately, people want to call the shots for their own lives. They want to keep that relationship or that lifestyle or that behavior.

From this point on the Jews plotted to put Jesus to death. The rationale of Caiaphas sounded to them like good situational ethics.

The Jewish leaders portray a classic example of what Jesus taught on another occasion: "If a person seeks to save his life, in the end he will lose it" (see Matt. 16:25). The Jewish leaders did exactly that: they tried to save their position. But in the end, they lost it. About forty years after Jesus' time, the Romans came and totally decimated the temple and the city of Jerusalem, and the survivors were led away to captivity. Had the Jews embraced Jesus as the Messiah, what they were so afraid of never would have happened. But in rejecting Him, the very thing they feared came upon them.

 APPLICATION

 PRAYER

Even as believers, we sometimes hold tightly to things that are precious to us—relationships, attitudes, positions. Even if the things we love are naturally good, grasping them can bring damage or even destruction to our lives. Will you ask Jesus to help you lay aside your autonomy completely and to be yielded to Him in every area of your life?

Lord, help us to see Your works and hear Your words and to infer from them that You are the Messiah—You are the Lord. Help us to let go of the worthless things we try to grasp and to embrace Jesus instead. We want the fullness of Your life. In Jesus' name. Amen.

SEEING ETERNITY

The world around us—that we can see and touch—seems very real to us. But the Bible tells us that there is another world that will last forever. How do we move our focus from this temporary world to the real, eternal one?

In this final week of Jesus' public ministry, the Lord attended a supper in the town of Bethany, the home of Lazarus, Mary, and Martha. During the meal, Mary approached Jesus with a bottle of expensive perfumed oil. She poured the oil on Jesus' feet and wiped His feet with her hair, "and the house was filled with the fragrance of the oil" (12:3). Mary's behavior wasn't standard protocol, but she wasn't concerned about that. She was expressing her deep love for Jesus.

Jesus' disciples still did not understand that Jesus was about to die, let alone be buried. Judas actually saw Mary's offering as a waste. *I could have had a piece of that,* he thought. But Mary had an insight into what was going on that the apostles didn't. "Leave her alone," Jesus said. "She has done this in preparation for My burial."

Mary's sensitivity was due to more than the fact that she was a woman. She was spiritually sensitive because every time she had a chance, she was focused on Jesus. Her habit of sitting at Jesus' feet had developed Mary's spiritual sensitivity to the point that she was the only one who realized Jesus was about to die.

The day after the supper, Jesus prepared to enter Jerusalem. When the people who had arrived for the Passover heard that Jesus was coming, they took palm branches, and as Jesus entered Jerusalem on a donkey, they cried out, "Hosanna! 'Blessed is He who comes in the name of the Lord!' The King of Israel!" (12:13).

Jesus had always downplayed His identity, but now, for the first time, He allowed this public display of His messiahship. This was His appointed time. At the wedding in Cana, He had said, "*My hour* has not yet come" (John 2:4). Now, as He entered Jerusalem, He said, "The hour has come that the Son of Man should be glorified" (12:23). Jesus had known all along that everything was moving toward this climax, during which He would glorify the Father by offering up His life for the sin of the world.

Amid the crowd's excitement, Jesus reminded His disciples of the spiritual reality taking place: "He who loves his life will lose it, and he who hates his life in this world will keep it for eternal life" (12:25).

Did Jesus mean that we are to think, *I hate myself; I'm ugly and fat and dumb?* Certainly not. Jesus meant that we must relinquish our life—we must let it go. Jim Elliot, a young missionary who, with four friends, gave his life to bring the gospel to the Waodoni Indians of Ecuador, said it well: "He is no fool who gives what he cannot keep to gain what he cannot lose."[4]

Jesus lived every day of His life on earth in view of another world: the real world, the eternal world. This is the world that Mary saw and Judas despised. Our world is temporary, although it constantly seeks to make us think that it is permanent.

When we are first saved, the reality of eternity is at the forefront of our minds, but as time passes and we get caught up in the busyness of life, sometimes that reality becomes dimmer. In His grace and mercy, God at times intervenes and reminds His people that He is alive, that He is working. He did that in a major way in Southern California in the early 1970s. And we pray that He will do it again.

We need to be like Mary—sitting at the feet of Jesus, taking in His Word. It is there that our eyes and our hearts will be opened to the things of eternity.

 APPLICATION

 PRAYER

How is your time with the Lord? If you have become too busy with activities and need a fresh reminder of spiritual realities, let go of anything that is cluttering your life, and become more like Mary, taking every opportunity to sit at Jesus' feet.

Lord, the material world is vying for our affection and is in many ways a mirage. Help us to sit at Your feet, to love Your presence, and to love Your Word that we may live for the eternal world. In Jesus' name. Amen.

FEARING GOD INSTEAD OF MEN

Have you ever been afraid to make a stand for Jesus because of how someone else might react? It's normal to feel fear in the face of opposition, but we should never seek people's approval more than God's.

Jesus, as we have seen, had done many signs to prove that He was the Messiah. Despite this, the spiritual leaders of Jerusalem flatly rejected Jesus. Tragically, because the Jews stubbornly persisted in rejecting Jesus Christ, God finally blinded their eyes and hardened their hearts.

Why would God intentionally do that? Because when someone insists on rejecting Him, in spite of the many proofs of His goodness and love, God finally confirms them in their choice. This is much like Pharaoh refusing again and again to free the Israelites (see Ex. 5–12).

Still, even among the Jewish leaders, it was obvious to many that Jesus was the Christ, as it had been to Nicodemus. He had said to Jesus, "We know that You are a teacher come from God; for no one can do these signs that You do unless God is with him" (John 3:2). But here is the tragedy: these believers did not confess Jesus for fear that they would be put out of the synagogue.

There are people today who know that Jesus is the Son of God, yet they do the same thing. They refuse to confess Him publicly for fear of losing friends or a position. Jesus said, "Whoever confesses Me before men, him I will also confess before My Father who is in heaven. But whoever denies Me before men, him I will also deny before My Father who is in heaven" (Matt. 10:32–33). The Jews refused to acknowledge Jesus because "they loved the praise of men more than the praise of God" (12:43).

When I became a Christian, the reputation I had among the guys I worked with suddenly changed. "Here comes preacher man," they'd say. "He has his radio again. He's going to make us listen to all those preachers." They hassled me all the time. Thankfully, I didn't care.

We should never let what others think determine whether or not we are going to follow the Lord. Through the prophet Isaiah, the Lord asked the people, in essence, "Why do you fear a man who will die?" (see Isa. 2:22). Those people who mock and ridicule us will stand before God in judgment. The world's hold on us can be powerful, but it's foolish for us to let another person's opinion determine our eternal destiny.

Jesus' final words to the Jews were sobering: "He who rejects Me, and does not receive My words, has that which judges him—the word that I have spoken will judge him in the last day" (12:48). Jesus didn't come to condemn; He came to save. But His word of salvation will also be a word of judgment in the final day. People will say, "I didn't know," or "I was afraid," and God will simply remind them of all the times people witnessed to them, all the times they sat in church, all the times they knew in their spirits that what they heard was true. The words they heard will be the words that condemn them.

At a certain point, since Israel counted themselves unworthy of eternal life, the gospel went to the Gentiles. That can happen to individuals when God extends His invitation to people over and over but they repeatedly turn Him down. We must never allow the fear of man to keep us from following Jesus or declaring Him to others. Our own eternity and that of others depends on it.

 APPLICATION

The Scripture says, "Today, if you will hear His voice, 'do not harden your heart'" (Ps. 95:7-8). Do you ever let fear of others dictate how you live when it comes to following Jesus? Ask the Lord for the courage to follow Him boldly, no matter what others think. The praise of God is worth infinitely more than the praise of men.

 PRAYER

Father, You are not willing that any should perish but that all should come to repentance. When Israel counted themselves unworthy of eternal life, the gospel went to the Gentiles. Let that not be the case with us individually. Help us never to be fearful of man but to boldly follow after You, that our lives will bring praise to the name of Jesus. Amen.

A NEW COMMANDMENT

Our natural inclination is to look out for number one. Even as believers, we tend to get offended when someone takes advantage of us or tries to get ahead of us. But Jesus' kingdom is upside down—the leader becomes the servant.

Jesus knew that His hour had come and that His remaining time with the disciples was short. At the final Passover meal that He shared with them, Jesus, God the Son, laid aside His garments, girded Himself with a towel, and began to wash His disciples' feet.

During the meal a dispute had arisen among the disciples over which of them would be greatest in the kingdom (see Luke 22:24). As the disciples observed Jesus and wondered what He was doing, perhaps their argument died down.

Jesus, of course, was painting a picture of our need to be cleansed by Him. But He was also setting an example for His disciples: "If I then, your Lord and Teacher, have washed your feet, you also ought to wash one another's feet" (13:14). The disciples esteemed the idea of ruling over others, but Jesus told them, "If you want to be great, learn to be the servant of all" (see Matt. 20:25-27). These men were going to be leaders in the church, and Jesus sought to instill this attitude of humility in their hearts.

As He taught, Jesus became troubled. "One of you," He told His followers, "will betray Me" (13:21). Judas, extremely clever, had kept his agenda hidden from the other disciples. As Jesus handed a piece of bread to Judas to indicate His betrayer, Judas "went out immediately. And it was night" (13:30). Earlier Jesus had said, "I must work while it is day, for the night is coming" (see John 9:4). The night had arrived.

Jesus now zeroed in on what He wanted the remaining eleven to grasp: "A new commandment I give to you, that you love one another" (13:34). Jesus was telling His followers, "Serve each other as I served you tonight. Don't fight for power. Give your lives for one another." By this kind of love, everyone would know that they were His disciples.

This has been one of the great failures of God's people throughout the ages. There has been so much bickering and hostility in the church, even hatred at times. In seeing that behavior, many people haven't taken Christianity seriously. In his book, *The God Delusion*, Richard Dawkins, renowned atheist, attacks God and the Christian faith. Sadly, a lot of his ammunition was taken from church history and the failure of Christians to love each other.

Some things we need to fight for, such as unbelief and sin, but we are never to fight each other. Even if someone won't reciprocate our love, we need to love him or her from a distance. The world can't argue with genuine love.

Peter, pondering Jesus' sobering words, interrupted Him. "Lord, where are You going? Why can't I follow You? I'm willing to lay down my life for You." Peter meant it. But like so many of us, Peter didn't know himself too well. "Really?" Jesus replied. "Before the night is over, you will deny that you know Me" (see John 13:36-38). The Bible warns us, "Let him who thinks he stands take heed lest he fall" (1 Cor. 10:12). Peter thought he was strong, but he was weak. Only when we recognize that we are weak and totally dependent on Christ will we be able to love Him, and others, as He asks us to.

The world tells us to love ourselves. But what it doesn't tell us is that selfishness is miserable. We are to love each other, to serve each other—even to the point of laying down our lives. When we serve God and serve His people, we find joy, peace, and fulfillment. When we lose our life, we find it.

 APPLICATION

Is there anyone toward whom you have anger, hurt, or unforgiveness? Cry out to God to teach you how to be the servant of all. Like Peter did, we need His strength to be holy. As God works in you, the world will know that you are a Christian by the love you have for others.

 PRAYER

Lord, thank You that You modeled for us the way of life and then called us to follow in Your steps. Help us to be done with living for ourselves and to live instead for You. Help us to love and serve one another, to lay down our lives for each other, and to find joy in doing so. In Jesus' name. Amen.

LET NOT YOUR HEART BE TROUBLED

We see many troubling things in the world today. Perhaps you see them in your own home, among your family members, or in your own life. Jesus has a remedy for our troubled hearts.

Jesus was now hours away from His trial, crucifixion, and death. As He shared the Last Supper with the men He had handpicked to be His apostles, He gave them difficult news. The disciples had expected the messianic kingdom to be inaugurated any day, but Jesus now made it very clear to them that He would be leaving. But Jesus encouraged them, "Let not your heart be troubled" (14:1).

The disciples *were* troubled. But the Lord had a reason for leaving: "I go to prepare a place for you. And if I go and prepare a place for you, I will come again and receive you to Myself; that where I am, there you may be also" (14:2-3). But all the disciples could see was that they would be separated from the Lord.

My wife and I live with a permanent ache because some of our children live far away from us. But in the few times each year when the whole family comes home, we are full of excitement because the family is together. The Father's house will be like that. All God's people throughout the ages will dwell together in perfect harmony. What a wonderful promise! When we see the insanity in the world around us, we must not be gripped by anxiety. Our citizenship is in heaven.

"You know the way to where I am going," Jesus told His followers. Thomas, a straightforward guy, spoke up. "Lord, we don't know where You are going, so how can we know the way?"

Jesus answered him, "I am the way, the truth, and the life. No one comes to the Father except through Me" (14:6). Here is Jesus' sixth "I am" statement and one of the greatest declarations ever made. Where was Jesus going? To the Father. And what is the way to the Father? Jesus told His disciples, "I am the way to the Father—the only way."

For many centuries in the Western world, people have more or less accepted Christian doctrine. If we state today, however, that Jesus is the only way to God, it produces a threatening situation. But Jesus is indeed the way—the atoning sacrifice for our sins and the only way we can find forgiveness and eternal life. He is the truth—the ultimate and only reality. And He is the life—every living thing, visible and invisible, draws its physical and spiritual life from Jesus Christ.

Philip, who with the others still wasn't grasping all Jesus taught, said, "Lord, show us the Father." Jesus replied, "Have I been with you so long, and yet you have not known Me, Philip? He who has seen Me has seen the Father" (14:8-9).

We can only experience God through Jesus. The revelation of God to man has always been through God the Son. That is why Jesus could say, "Before Abraham was, I AM" (John 8:58), taking the very name by which God had revealed Himself to Moses at the burning bush. Only the person who has seen Jesus has seen the Father.

The years ahead will likely be more tumultuous than these recent years have been. But no secret coup will dethrone the Lord. The glorification of man and his rebellion and sin against God is broadcast here, there, and everywhere, and if we keep our attention on those things, we will be troubled. But if we take our eyes off what is happening around us and put them on Jesus, our hearts will be at rest.

 APPLICATION

 PRAYER

Is your heart troubled over things taking place in our country? In the world? In your personal life? Let not your heart be troubled. Believe in Jesus. He is the way to heaven, and that's where we are going. Put your eyes on Jesus and believe Him to show you the way.

Lord, You are the way, the truth, and the life. Thank You that we can rest in You because You have everything under control. We know that You are preparing a place for us in Your Father's house and that You will come again to receive us to Yourself. Help us to live in anticipation of Your return, and when our hearts are troubled, may we put our trust in You. In Jesus' name. Amen.

PREPARATION FOR SERVICE

Even the smartest, most energetic, most creative person needs more than his own abilities to be spiritually effective. Serving God requires a totally different kind of power—the power of the Holy Spirit.

These eleven faithful men who had traveled and ministered with Jesus had watched the Lord do many amazing miracles. Now Jesus told them that those who believed in Him would do even greater works than He had done. What did Jesus mean?

As we look at the early church in the book of Acts and at church history throughout the ages, we don't see anybody doing works that were qualitatively greater than the works of Jesus. The Lord was saying that the quantity, not the quality, of the disciples' works would be greater than His. Jesus' works had been limited by locality, since He was confined in a human body. But when Jesus left, the Father would send the Holy Spirit, and by the power of the Spirit in the disciples, the works of Jesus would be multiplied over and over in countless places (see Acts 1:8).

So that they would be able to carry out these works, Jesus told the disciples that the Father would give them "another Helper" (14:16). "Another" in the original language means "another of the same kind." The Helper, the Holy Spirit, would be just like Jesus. On their own, the disciples were prone to failure, but empowered by the Holy Spirit, they would be able to minister with authority and fruitfulness.

The Spirit of God, Jesus told the disciples, had actually been with them for some time. When Jesus had sent them out two by two to minister, the disciples had healed the sick, raised the dead, and cast out demons by the Spirit (see Mark 6:7-13). But Jesus now told His followers, "He will be *in* you."

In a sense, all of us have had the Spirit *with* us. Before we came to Christ, the Spirit came alongside us and began to prod us, letting us know that we were sinners and needed a Savior.

When we responded to His prompting and asked Jesus to forgive our sins, the Holy Spirit began to dwell *in* us. The Holy Spirit indwells every true believer in Jesus Christ.

"If anyone does not have the Spirit of Christ, he is not His" (Rom. 8:9). The Holy Spirit comes to dwell in us to give us the life of God—to save us.

Yet, there is a third experience of the Holy Spirit not mentioned in this conversation between Jesus and His disciples: His coming *upon* us. Jesus referred to this earlier when He cried, "He who believes in Me ... out of his heart will flow rivers of living water" (John 7:38). And later Jesus would tell His followers, "You shall receive power when the Holy Spirit has come upon you" (Acts 1:8). The Holy Spirit comes upon us to give us spiritual power to serve God that His life might pour out onto others and they too be filled with the Spirit.

The disciples would need this empowering, because Jesus told them, "If anyone loves Me, he will keep My word" (14:23). To simply say that we love God is not sufficient. We need to obey—and we can only do this with the help of the Holy Spirit.

As Jesus prepared the disciples for His calling on their lives, they were likely somewhat overwhelmed. But He reminded them again, "Peace I leave with you ... let not your heart be troubled, neither let it be afraid" (14:27). They were about to face cataclysmic changes, but in the power of the Holy Spirit, they would do mighty works that would affect the entire world for the kingdom of God.

 APPLICATION

 PRAYER

Are you leaning on your own energy and abilities to serve the Lord, or are you serving Christ in the power of the Holy Spirit? If you lack passion and power in your life or ministry, simply pray, "Lord, fill me," so that the Holy Spirit can overflow from your life and use you powerfully for His kingdom.

Thank You, Lord, for calling us to serve You. Thank You for sending the Holy Spirit to enable us to keep Your commands and walk in Your power. Fill us with Your Holy Spirit, we pray, and empower us so that people around us will come to know You. Use our lives for the Father's glory, as You used the disciples. In Jesus' name. Amen.

ABIDING IN CHRIST

Sometimes we get too busy to seek the Lord. We may read our Bibles a bit each day, but we fail to saturate ourselves in the Word. In times like these, love, joy, peace, and patience are hard to come by. The Lord intends better for His followers.

Jesus and His disciples had left the upper room, where they had shared a final meal and had begun moving toward the Mount of Olives. Jesus, knowing that His imminent trial, judgment, and death had the potential to rock the disciples' faith, continued speaking to them, preparing these eleven men to remain strong in Him through the changes about to come.

"I am the true vine" (15:1), He began. This is the seventh and final instance in which the Lord used this "I am" formula, identifying Himself again as the God of Israel. Then He spoke a phrase that He would repeat over and over: "Abide in Me" (15:4). By "abide" the Lord meant "live." We are to live in Christ in the same way that a branch is connected to the vine. This union is essential since a branch cannot exist apart from the vine.

Jesus made a big deal of this because He wants His people to bear fruit. Galatians 5:22-23 tells us that the fruit God wants in our lives is the fruit of the Holy Spirit—love, joy, peace, patience, and other qualities that reflect the character of Christ. Sadly, many people in the church do not bear this kind of fruit because they are not abiding in the vine—they don't have a vital union with Jesus Christ.

Jesus told His disciples that His Father, the vinedresser, would remove every branch that did not bear fruit. This is exactly what happened to Israel historically. Israel refused to believe in Jesus, and many thousands of Jews were taken into captivity a few decades after they rejected the Messiah.

The branches that remained, however—those who believed in Christ—would be pruned so that they might bear more fruit. Being pruned isn't fun. Sometimes it comes in the form of difficulties that we experience. Other times it comes as we read God's Word and the Lord exposes things in us that He wants to get rid of. But this cleansing process is necessary if we are going to be healthy and fruitful.

Abiding is simple. To abide we just need to keep believing in Jesus. Stay close to Him. Spend time with Him. Obey Him. "If you keep My commandments," Jesus said, "you will abide in My love" (15:10).

Jesus, as He had done earlier, impressed one command in particular upon His disciples: "This is My commandment, that you love one another as I have loved you" (15:12). More than any other, the fruit Jesus wants to see in our lives is love for each other. It's not always easy to love, but Jesus showed us how to do it: "Greater love has no one than this, than to lay down one's life for his friends" (15:13). We love people by laying down our lives for them, just as Jesus did for us. Giving up our rights. Letting go of our hurts. This is abiding in Christ.

If we obey Jesus' commands, if we abide in Him, the Lord calls us His friends. Amazing!

God's main purpose in creating Adam and Eve was to have communion with them. When sin came in, their relationship was broken, but Jesus' death on the cross repaired the damaged relationship between God and man. So many people think of Christianity as a list of rules to obey, but Jesus wants to be our friend.

God wants us to be so connected to Him that He can flow through us just as the life of a vine flows through its branches. He wants kindness, gentleness, and humility to flow from us to others. This is the natural result of abiding in Jesus.

 APPLICATION

 PRAYER

What kind of fruit comes from your life? Holiness, love, and peace? Or irritation, frustration, even anger? If you need fresh fruit in your life, start abiding in Jesus—spend time in His presence, fill yourself with His Word. His joy and peace and kindness will fill you and flow from you and will draw others to Christ.

Lord, it is wonderfully amazing that You chose us and want to be our friends. Help us to abide in You in the deepest sense, to live in You and obey You so that our lives will be fruitful for Your kingdom. In Jesus' name. Amen.

BE OF GOOD CHEER

Early in His ministry Jesus had taught His disciples, "Blessed are you when they revile and persecute you. Rejoice and be exceedingly glad" (Matt. 5:11–12). Seems like a contradiction in terms, doesn't it? How does a person rejoice in persecution?

Jesus, continuing His final, very personal conversation with His apostles, was preparing to send them into the world to spread the gospel. The disciples still hadn't fully grasped the messianic mission, and Jesus was about to break more difficult news to them: as they carried out their mission, the world would hate them.

"But remember," Jesus told them, "it hated Me first." It is mind-boggling that people could hate Jesus Christ, a Man who did good and healed the oppressed (see Acts 10:38). But Jesus explained it: "[The world] hates Me because I testify of it that its deeds are evil" (John 7:7). This is why Israel's religious leaders, these men who were supposed to lead people to God, were filled with hatred for Him. From the outset of our relationship with Jesus, we need to recognize that people, even at times those who claim to follow God, will be hostile toward us because they are hostile toward Him.

Jesus reminded His disciples again that He would be leaving and that they would remain to bear witness of Him to the world. But, as Jesus had been, they would be opposed: "They will put you out of the synagogues; yes, the time is coming that whoever kills you will think that he offers God service" (16:2). Much of the persecution against believers throughout the centuries has been led by people who claimed to be believers themselves. For the disciples it was the Jewish leaders; later in history it was the established church. But ultimately, Jesus said, those who do these things "have not known the Father nor Me" (16:3). Those who committed atrocities in the Crusades or the Inquisition were not Christians. Christians love their enemies. They do good. They bless.

As the disciples began to grasp what Jesus was saying, their hearts, understandably, were filled with sorrow. But Jesus consoled them, "It is to your advantage that I go away; for if I do not go away, the Helper will not come to you" (16:7). The disciples couldn't conceive of Jesus' leaving being an advantage to them. But as long as Jesus was on earth, the Holy Spirit would not be poured out.

Jesus spoke these difficult things to His disciples to prepare them for the work of taking the message of salvation to the whole world. The Holy Spirit would help them in this task, just as He helps the church today, by convicting people of sin, righteousness, and judgment.

Jesus had more to tell the disciples, but He knew that they could not bear it all. Only later, through the Holy Spirit's teaching, would the disciples finally understand the significance of Jesus' life, death, and resurrection. But Jesus told His disciples certain things so that when events took place, the disciples would remember Jesus' words and be encouraged in their call to take the gospel to the ends of the earth. Jesus gives us the same word He gave His disciples: "In the world you will have tribulation; but be of good cheer, I have overcome the world" (16:33).

The world will be hostile toward God until Jesus comes again and establishes His kingdom. This is the environment in which we live and function and, helped by the Holy Spirit, take the gospel to the world. The news media bombards us daily with many reasons for concern, but we must not be overcome by anxiety and fear. In this world we will have tribulation, but Jesus has overcome the world.

 APPLICATION

 PRAYER

Are you of good cheer? Are you filled with joy and strength in the work of the kingdom of God? You can be! Let go of discouraging thoughts. Set aside depressing news and pessimistic outlooks. The events happening around us only confirm that what Jesus told His followers is true. This should strengthen our faith and make us even bolder to take the gospel to the world.

Lord, thank You for telling us in advance what will take place so that we can be strong in times of trial and persecution. Thank You for pouring out Your Holy Spirit to help us take the gospel to the world. Make us strong disciples of Jesus in the face of opposition so that Your name will be glorified and many will come to know You. In Jesus' name. Amen.

IN THE WORLD BUT NOT OF IT

In a society that is increasingly hostile to God, being a Christian isn't always easy. And it's going to get harder. Why doesn't God take us directly to heaven when we are saved to spare us all this difficulty?

Jesus had washed His disciples' feet. He had told these men that He was leaving and that the Holy Spirit was coming. He had told them that the world would hate them, and He had encouraged them to "be of good cheer" (16:33). Now Jesus began to pray.

"Father," He began, "the hour has come" (17:1)—the hour in which He would be glorified on the cross, the ultimate task for which He had been sent into the world. For three years Jesus had offered the people of Israel eternal life, and now He prayed, "I have finished the work which You have given Me to do" (17:4). He looked forward to sharing once again in His Father's glory.

Jesus, knowing that His disciples would remain in the hostile environment of the world, began to pray for these men. "I have manifested Your name to the men whom You have given Me" (17:6), Jesus prayed. When Jesus came, people had been confused about God's nature. Jesus had brought to His disciples and to Israel—and to us—a clear picture of who God is. Jesus had made God's love and power and salvation known.

Now Jesus was about to leave His followers with their newfound knowledge of the Father and return to heaven. "Holy Father," He continued, "keep through Your name those whom You have given Me" (17:11). The disciples would remain in enemy territory—the world system that lives in rebellion against God. Jesus prayed that the dangers of this fallen world would not sweep His followers away.

He prayed too that they would be protected from the directed, calculated strategy of our great adversary, Satan: "I do not pray that You should take them out of the world, but that You should keep them from the evil one" (17:15). God allows Satan to have a certain freedom with us so that He can work things into us that wouldn't be implanted any other way. But the Devil can't do anything to us that the Lord doesn't allow. None of us is a match for the Devil, but he is no match for the Lord.

Why does God leave us in this sin-saturated world? One reason is that He wants to use this life to sanctify us: "Sanctify them by Your truth" (17:17), Jesus prayed. The word "sanctify" means simply "to set apart." Jesus was praying that His people would be set apart for God. He does this by His truth—His Word. With sin all around us, and inside us, we must immerse ourselves in the truth of God's Word in order to guard against carnality. Every mature, Spirit-filled Christian on the planet has a serious relationship with the Word of God.

Now Jesus prayed for us: "I do not pray for these alone," Jesus went on, "but also for those who will believe in Me through their word; that they all may be one, as You, Father, are in Me, and I in You" (17:20–21). Even when we don't behave as if we are, all true believers in Christ are one. Christ is in us. The Father is in Christ. Christ is in me, and Christ is in you. We have an undeniable and unbreakable unity amid the animosity of this world.

The world holds many dangers, toils, and snares that could sweep us away from the Lord. But Jesus prayed that while we are *in* the world, we would not be *of* the world. We are here for a reason: God is training us, growing us in Him so that we will be ready for the life to come.

 ## APPLICATION

 ## PRAYER

In what ways are you tempted by the world? How might the enemy be attacking you right now? If you are struggling, be encouraged. The Lord has His eye on you. He is using your difficulties to make you more like Him and to prepare you for eternity.

Lord Jesus, thank You for praying that we would be kept in this sin-cursed world and guarded from the evil one, that we would be sanctified and become one with You and with each other. We are grateful for the reminder that You are praying for us—and we know that Your prayers are being answered. We pray in Jesus' name. Amen.

FACE TO FACE WITH THE TRUTH

The truth exposes things. Because of this, not everyone likes it. People who came face-to-face with Jesus, the truth Himself, reacted in varying ways—most of them foolish. But the way we respond to the truth has huge ramifications for our lives.

Following the Last Supper, Jesus and His disciples had made their way to the Mount of Olives. As they spent their last moments together, here came troops and officers, sent by the religious leaders of Israel, to arrest the Lord.

"We're looking for Jesus of Nazareth," they said. Jesus responded, "I am He." Actually, in the original language, Jesus said simply, "I am," once again taking unto Himself that name by which God was recognized among the Jews. Notice the response. When Jesus spoke, the soldiers fell backward to the ground. It is amazing that they continued their pursuit.

Peter, of course, reacted. He drew his sword "and struck the high priest's servant, and cut off his right ear" (18:10). This was Jesus they were arresting. Peter's Messiah. But Jesus said to Peter, "Put your sword into the sheath. Shall I not drink the cup which My Father has given Me?" (18:11). The disciples wouldn't understand until later that all this was the fulfillment of prophecy.

The officers bound Jesus and led Him away to the high priest. Peter and "another disciple"—John, no doubt—followed. As the two approached the high priest's courtyard, Peter was about to be tested.

The servant girl at the door said to Peter, "You're not one of His disciples, are you?" Peter quickly replied, "I am not" (18:17). Once inside, Peter was asked twice more if he was a disciple of Jesus, and twice he firmly replied, "I am not!" (18:25). Luke's gospel tells us that at the moment Peter made his final denial, Jesus' eyes met Peter's (see Luke 22:61). We can imagine what went on in Peter's heart as he looked into the eyes of the Lord.

As the high priest and the other leaders questioned Jesus, an officer struck Him. This action was against Jewish law, yet the religious leaders, who had arrested Jesus for supposedly breaking the Law, violated the Law throughout their confrontation with Him.

The Jews led Jesus to the Praetorium—the home of the Roman governor, Pilate. "But they themselves did not go into the Praetorium, lest they should be defiled, but that they might eat the Passover" (18:28). These men had no problem seeking a death sentence for an innocent man but were concerned about being ceremonially defiled. What blindness.

Pilate questioned Jesus: "Are You a king?" (18:37). Jesus affirmed that He was, but He made it clear that His kingdom was not of this world. Jesus explained, "For this cause I was born, and for this cause I have come into the world, that I should bear witness to the truth. Everyone who is of the truth hears My voice" (18:37).

In our day the existence of truth is blatantly denied. People say that there is no absolute truth. Jesus told us not only that truth exists but that He Himself is the truth, a fact rejected by those Christians who have drifted into liberal philosophical and emergent views.

Pilate, an obvious skeptic, said to Jesus, "What is truth?" (18:38). Pilate could see that Jesus was not like the hypocritical religious leaders he so despised, but by this point he had become so disillusioned that, rather than inquiring further of Jesus, he seemed to have given up on the idea of truth entirely. Pilate knew that the Jewish leaders had delivered Jesus to him out of envy and that Jesus had done no wrong. Sadly, he was more concerned about his political well-being than the truth.

We too are confronted with the truth in the gospel of Jesus Christ, and it requires a response. What is the proper response? Ultimately, it is to receive Jesus Christ, the embodiment of the truth.

 APPLICATION

What response does the truth produce in you? The guards were knocked down. The Pharisees were hateful. Pilate was indifferent. Only Peter, stung to the heart by conviction, went on to respond rightly to the truth. What is Jesus saying to you today, and how will you respond?

 PRAYER

Thank You, Lord, that You are the truth. As the light of Your truth shines in our lives, may our hearts never be hard and angry but always soft and humble. Expose anything in us that needs to go so that we will be clean and free to serve You. We pray in Jesus' name. Amen.

IT IS FINISHED!

Have you ever stopped to consider how wonderful it is that Jesus took care of our sin once and for all? His forgiveness isn't temporary or incomplete. It is total! By Jesus' blood our sin is completely washed away. We must never take this lightly.

Pilate, reluctant to put Jesus to death, attempted to appease the Jews by ordering that Jesus be flogged. One can only imagine how ruthless the Roman soldiers were—scourging Him, mocking Him, pressing a crown of thorns into His head, striking Him, spitting on Him, even plucking out His beard (see Matt. 27:30; Mark 15:19; Isa. 50:6). Pilate presented Jesus' broken body to the Jews, appealing to any ounce of compassion they might have had. The Jewish leaders, unmoved, cried out, "Crucify Him!" (19:6).

Pilate, in a last effort, petitioned the Jews once more: "Shall I crucify your King?" The chief priests replied, "We have no king but Caesar!" (19:15). That statement sealed the doom of the Jewish nation. These men, speaking on behalf of all Israel, pledged their allegiance to Caesar and rejected the God they claimed to serve.

So Pilate gave Jesus up to be crucified. Jesus, carrying His own cross, was led to "the Place of a Skull" (19:17), and there He was crucified between two thieves.

As Jesus hung on the cross, the soldiers gambled for His clothing. At some point Jesus addressed His mother, Mary, and John, His faithful disciple, who stood together nearby: "Woman, behold your son!" and then to John, "Behold your mother!" (19:26-27). As the hours dragged on, "Jesus, knowing that all things were now accomplished, that the Scripture might be fulfilled, said, 'I thirst!'" (19:28).

Any Jewish person familiar with the Scriptures, as he observed this scene, would have flashed back to the Psalms. Psalm 22, which prophesies the death of the Messiah, says, "They pierced My hands and My feet," and "They divide My garments among them, and for My clothing they cast lots" (Ps. 22:16, 18). The other gospel writers tell us that Jesus cried out, "My God, My God, why have You forsaken Me?" a direct quote from Psalm 22:1 (see also Matt. 27:46). Jesus' statement about being thirsty was a reference to Psalm 69:21. Many prophecies were being fulfilled during Jesus' crucifixion even in these smallest details.

Those near Jesus lifted to Him a sponge soaked in sour wine, and when He had taken it, Jesus cried out, "'It is finished!' And bowing His head, He gave up His spirit" (19:30).

"It is finished." These words are full of meaning. Daniel 9:24 tells us that God had appointed a time "to finish the transgression, to make an end of sins … to bring in everlasting righteousness." This was that time.

The words can be translated "paid in full." Through sin we had sold ourselves to the Devil and to his tyranny over our lives, and to redeem us, Jesus, the innocent and righteous One, shed His blood and paid in full the price to bring us back to God and to deliver us from sin and the Devil. "It is finished" was His victory cry.

In the fulfillment of God's great plan, the price for our sin was paid in full. How do we celebrate with Jesus in His cry of victory? We commemorate Jesus' victory today by taking Communion—something Jesus told us to do in remembrance of Him (see 1 Cor. 11:23–25).

It is lamentably easy for us to forget what the Lord has done for us. Jesus knew this, and He told us, "Take the bread and the cup, and remember Me. Remember how I suffered for you, how I shed My blood and bore the shame. Remember My cry of victory: 'It is finished! The price is paid in full!'" May our hearts be so moved by Jesus' incomprehensible act of love that we worship and serve Him all our days.

 APPLICATION

The price for our sins has been paid in full! Does this move you to gratitude? To joy? To worship and service? If you have forgotten what Jesus has done for you, stop and remember Him once again. Let Him rekindle in you a heart of love and service for Him.

 PRAYER

Lord, our hearts tend to grow cold and hard. Sometimes we consider Your great act so lightly. Forgive us, Lord. May our hearts be tender! As we meditate upon Your body that was broken and Your blood that was shed, may we be deeply moved to love and to serve You. Thank You for Your unspeakable gift. In Jesus' name. Amen.

THAT YOU MAY BELIEVE

John wrote his gospel to convince people that Jesus is the Messiah so that they would believe in Him and thus have life. Many of us believe the gospel message, but at times we doubt God's Word to us regarding other matters. As we will see, Jesus honors our belief.

Early on the first day of the week, Mary Magdalene went to the tomb where the Lord had been laid. On her arrival she found that the large stone that had sealed the tomb had been rolled away. She ran to Peter and "the other disciple" (20:2), most certainly John, and told them that someone had taken Jesus' body.

Peter and John ran to the tomb. Peter, the original language tells us, simply "saw" that it was empty, but John "saw and perceived." The light went on. John suddenly realized that, just as He had said He would, Jesus had risen from the dead.

The disciples, once they realized that Jesus was now resurrected, most likely expected that, finally, He would go to Jerusalem, pronounce Himself Messiah, and set up His kingdom. But God had a different plan.

That evening the disciples were gathered behind locked doors, legitimately afraid that they might be rounded up and executed as Jesus had been. At this point only Mary and two other disciples had seen the resurrected Jesus (see Luke 24:35). Suddenly Jesus appeared in their midst and said, "Peace be with you" (20:19).

This gathering was made up not only of the apostles but of all those who had been with Jesus, including a number of women. In a sense, this was the first gathering of the church. What Jesus told them was not for a select few but for the body of Christ: "As the Father has sent Me, I also send you" (20:21). The Father had sent Jesus into the world to redeem mankind, and now Jesus was sending His church into the world to preach the gospel.

After He commissioned them, Jesus "breathed on them, and said to them, 'Receive the Holy Spirit'" (20:22). Way back at the creation of the world, God had first breathed into man the breath of life (see Gen. 2:7), but when Adam and Eve disobeyed God, man died spiritually. As Jesus breathed on His followers, He recreated man. In that instant they were indwelt by the Spirit—regenerated, brought back to life, born again.

Thomas, one of the eleven, was not present at this gathering. That was one meeting he should not have missed! The others told him that they had seen the Lord, but Thomas didn't believe it. "Unless I see in His hands the print of the nails, and put my finger into the print of the nails, and put my hand into His side, I will not believe" (20:25).

Eight days later the disciples were together again, and this time Thomas was with them. Suddenly Jesus appeared and spoke to Thomas: "Touch My hands, and put your finger in My side. Don't be unbelieving, but believing" (20:27).

"My Lord and My God!" Thomas replied (20:28). Jesus had claimed in many ways to be God. Now He again showed His claim to deity by accepting Thomas's declaration.

"Because you have seen Me, you have believed," Jesus told him. "Blessed are those who have not seen and yet have believed" (20:29). This was a rebuke for Thomas, but it is a word of blessing to those throughout history who have not seen Jesus but have believed the testimony of God's Word.

John's purpose in writing his gospel was that we might believe: "These are written that you may believe that Jesus is the Christ, the Son of God, and that believing you may have life in His name" (20:31). God reserves a special blessing for those who believe in Him without having seen Him. May we not be unbelieving, but believing.

 ## APPLICATION

Even as believers, we sometimes doubt God. We just can't believe that He will do what He promised to do. Will you believe only what you can see, or will you believe the promises of God? As you believe the Lord, you will experience life in His name.

 ## PRAYER

Lord, how we thank You for this great gospel that so enriches and blesses us. Let us not be like Thomas. We haven't seen You, but we believe in You. John wrote his gospel so that people would believe in You—use us as well to help people believe in You. Embolden Your church in these days. In Jesus' name. Amen.

RESTORED AND RECOMMISSIONED

Despite our intentions to please the Lord, we all fail to one degree or another. But if we truly repent of our sin, God graciously allows us to keep serving Him—even when we can think of a hundred reasons He should not.

The disciples, after Jesus had twice appeared to them, made their way north to Galilee to resume their lives. Jesus had apparently vanished, so they went fishing.

After fishing all night, they'd caught nothing. A man on the shore called out to them, "Cast your net on the right side of the boat!" They did so, and their net became so full that they could not draw it in. John, "that disciple whom Jesus loved," said to Peter, "It is the Lord!" (21:7). Peter, always impetuous, plunged into the water and swam for shore.

When they arrived at the shore, "they saw a fire of coals there, and fish laid on it, and bread" (21:9). The last time Peter and the Lord had talked, Peter told Jesus, "I'm willing to die for You!" But Peter, under pressure, had denied that he knew the Lord—three times. Few of us can fully imagine the anguish of soul Peter had gone through.

After they ate Jesus spoke directly to Simon Peter: "Simon, son of Jonah, do you love Me more than these?" (21:15). Some have suggested that "these" meant the fish—in other words, Peter's livelihood. Yet I believe that Jesus was speaking of the other disciples: "Do you love Me more than the other disciples do?" Peter had earlier intimated that he did (see Matt. 26:33). He had obviously been mistaken.

When Jesus asked, "Do you love Me?" He used the Greek word *agape*: "Do you agape Me? Do you love Me with a deep, loyal, complete type of love?" Peter answered Jesus, "Yes, Lord; You know that I love You" (21:15), but he used the Greek word *phileo*, "to be fond of." "Yes, Lord," he said, probably hanging his head a bit, "You know that I am fond of You."

Jesus repeated His question. "Peter, do you agape Me?" Peter replied a second time, "Lord, I phileo You."

When Jesus asked a third time, He came down to Peter's level. "Simon," He said, "do you phileo Me? Are you fond of Me?" At times, amazingly, the Lord in His love condescends to our weakness. Peter was grieved at the third question, but it broke him of his self-confidence.

Jesus questioned Peter three times—the same number of times Peter had denied Him. At the Last Supper Jesus had told Peter, "Satan has desired to sift you as wheat, but I have prayed for you" (see Luke 22:31–32). Satan had sifted him. Peter had failed. But Jesus restored him. God is in the business of restoration.

But Jesus did more than restore Peter. He recommissioned him. After He freed Peter from condemnation, Jesus told him, "Look, Peter, it's not over. Feed My sheep." Peter was to feed the newborn church the Word of God and to nurture the believers.

Jesus had sobering news for Peter as well: one day he would give his life for his faith. On hearing this Peter looked at John and said, "What about him?" Basically Jesus politely told Peter, and He tells us as well, "Mind your own business." Our part is simply to follow Jesus, even if His path for us is a rough road or different than others.

After this Peter was fine. He served Jesus, and he followed Him—to the end. Church history tells us that Peter was crucified in Rome, upside down at his own request because he did not feel worthy to be crucified in the same manner Jesus had been.

When we fail, God is ready to forgive us and to restore us to His service. As we step into God's will for our lives, let us keep focused on His calling. As we follow Jesus, God will accomplish His specific purpose in and through each of us.

 APPLICATION

 PRAYER

Are you fully yielded to the Lord? Are you willing to follow Him, no matter the cost? If you are, say to Him, "Lord, here I am. Take me and use me. Fulfill Your purpose in me, and be glorified in my life."

Thank You, Lord, for the gospel of John. And thank You for Your grace that restores and recommissions us. Help us to focus on Your calling for our lives and be glorified in us in these days. In Jesus' name. Amen.

CONCLUSION

THAT PEOPLE MAY HAVE LIFE

These are written that you may believe that Jesus is the Christ, the Son of God,
and that believing you may have life in His name.
John 20:31

Jesus, the Word of God, had approximately three years of public ministry in which to bring the knowledge of God to the Jews. Many things that Jesus said and did during those years are not recorded. The Gospels are not exhaustive, nor were they intended to be. They do not present a full history, although they are historically accurate. The primary objective of the Gospels is that we might know who Jesus is and put our faith in Him.

As John closes his gospel, he writes, "There are also many other things that Jesus did, which if they were written one by one, I suppose that even the world itself could not contain the books that would be written" (21:25). John could have told us much more about the things that Jesus did, but the apostle, led by the Spirit, had a specific purpose in writing his gospel: that people would believe that Jesus is the Christ, the Son of the living God, and that by believing they would have life in His name. As followers of Jesus, our lives should reflect the same goal.

In the introduction to this book, I mentioned a phenomenon that has occurred in our society in recent years: people like Jesus, but they don't like the church. If we as Christians truly know Jesus, if we are filled with His life, then our lives and our churches will attract people, not repel them. It is my prayer that through this devotional you have seen Jesus in a fresh way and that His life in you is more visible to the world than ever before.

I am always on the lookout for a good gospel tract, but I believe that the best gospel tract we could give anybody is the gospel of John. It was written for the very purpose that we have in evangelizing: to convince people that Jesus is the Messiah, the Savior of the world, so that they will believe in Him and experience life in His name.

When we share Christ with people, it is vitally important that we give them the historical account of the gospel. Take them back to Genesis—back to the beginning, as John did (see John 1:1–5). Did God promise a Redeemer, or didn't He? We can tell people that Jesus said, "I am the way, the truth and the life. No one comes to the Father except through Me" (John 14:6), but we need to state it in its historical context because a lot of religions make similar statements.

In the beginning God created man, but shortly afterward, fellowship between God and man was broken through sin. God promised to restore that fellowship through a Redeemer when He pronounced punishment on Satan: "I will put enmity between you and the woman, and between your seed and her Seed; He shall bruise your head, and you shall bruise His heel" (Gen. 3:15). Jesus is the culmination of God's plan of redemption. Jesus is the way, the truth, and the life, and no one comes to the Father except through Him, because He is the One whom God promised to the first two people back in the garden.

Today, we live in a multiethnic, multicultural society. People come to us from all over the world, having different traditions and religions. Many of them have never heard of Jesus. When we make the true claim to them that Jesus is the only way, we need to put it in context.

This is why John wrote his gospel. He was showing us that Jesus is the Christ. The Messiah. The long-awaited Savior of the world. The One whom God promised Adam and Eve that He would send.

Do you know Jesus? Are you trusting Him, abiding in Him, drawing life from Him? If you are, then the world will be able to tell. They will see your servant's heart, your love for other believers, your love for the lost. They will see Jesus in you. Ask the Lord for a fresh impartation of His Holy Spirit upon you, and go out each day, encouraged and unafraid in the power of the Spirit, that the people around you may believe in Jesus and have life in His name.

RECOMMENDED RESOURCES

If this devotional has ministered to you, you may be encouraged by reading or studying more resources that will help you go deeper in your relationship with Jesus. The following recommendations are based on quotes and contents from *When God Became One of Us*.

Calvary Chapel Resources

Brian Brodersen's sermons, books, and videos: www.backtobasicsradio.com

Chuck Smith's "Through the Bible" series sermons: www.twft.com

More Resources

John Bunyan, *Pilgrim's Progress*.

Charles Spurgeon, *Morning and Evening*. New Kensington, PA: Whitaker, 1997.

Elisabeth Elliot, *Through Gates of Splendor*. Carol Stream, IL: Tyndale, 1981.

NOTES

[1] Jon Courson, *Jon Courson's Application Commentary: Volume 3, New Testament (Matthew - Revelation)* (Nashville, TN: Thomas Nelson, 2004).

[2] G. Campbell Morgan, *The Great Physician: The Method of Jesus with Individuals* (Eugene, OR: Wipf and Stock Publishers, 2010).

[3] Charles Spurgeon, *The Autobiography of Charles H. Spurgeon V1: 1834-1854* (Literary Licensing, LLC, August 7, 2014).

[4] Elisabeth Elliot, *Shadow Almighty: The Life and Testament of Jim Elliot* (Harper Collins, 2009).